HOW TO MAKE APPLIC
FAMILY PROCEEDI~~ ~~~ ~~~~~

A Step by Step Guide to the
Children Act in the Magistrates' Court

To the memory of Jack Sarch

HOW TO MAKE APPLICATIONS IN THE FAMILY PROCEEDINGS COURT

A Step by Step Guide to the Children Act in the Magistrates' Court

Paul Mallender LLB
of Lincoln's Inn, Barrister

Jane Rayson LLB
of Gray's Inn, Barrister

BLACKSTONE PRESS LIMITED

First published in Great Britain 1992 by Blackstone Press Limited,
9-15 Aldine Street, London W12 8AW. Telephone 081-740 1173

© P. Mallender and J. Rayson, 1992

ISBN: 1 85431 201 4

British Library Cataloguing in Publication Data
A CIP catalogue record for this book is available from the British Library

Typeset by: Style Photosetting, Mayfield, East Sussex
Printed by: Redwood Press Limited, Melksham

Contents

Families Need Fathers

Keeping Children and Parents in Contact   Registered Charity No.276899

134 Curtain Road, London EC2A 3AR   **0171 613 5060 / 0990 502 506**

Dear Mr. Leonard,

The other items ordered will follow under separate cover.

Regards,
Tim   24/2/99

With compliments

Preface

There are a number of excellent books on the Children Act 1989. They deal, however, almost exclusively with the substantive law.

This pocket-sized handbook provides for child care specialists and busy general practitioners alike, not only the essential elements of the new law, but also a handy guide to the new procedure.

Within its pages you will find the answers to practical questions such as:

(a)   How do I make my application?

(b)   Which forms do I fill in?

(c)   What should I put in my application?

(d)   Does my client need permission to make the application; if so how do I obtain the leave of the court?

(e)   Whom should I serve with the proceedings? How do I serve them?

(f)   Who is entitled to notice of the proceedings?

(g)   What are the new rules of evidence?

(h)   How should I prepare for the hearing?

(i)   Can I apply for directions and, if so, how?

(j)   Can the child apply for orders under the new legislation?

(k)   How can I enforce the orders I obtain?

Page references in this book are to the pages of the Family Proceedings Courts (Children Act 1989) Rules 1991, where readers will find the individual CHA Forms which are referred to in the text.

We have followed the scheme of the Act by referring to 'the child' throughout in the masculine. The masculine throughout also includes the feminine.

Paul Mallender
Jane Rayson
November 1991

Acknowledgments

To Zoe Kavadas for her typewriting skills (and patience!), to Andrea Rivers for her careful proof reading and to Elli Pearce for her elegant handwriting.

Thanks and acknowledgments are also due to the Controller of Her Majesty's Stationery Office for permission to reproduce the forms included in the text published under the Family Proceedings Court (Children Act 1989) Rules 1991, and to The Solicitors' Law Stationery Society Limited for permission to use the Oyez versions of the forms.

Chapter 1

Preliminaries

1.1 INTRODUCTION

All the applications considered in this book can be heard by the family proceedings court (formerly the domestic court within the magistrates' court), the county court, or the High Court. The applicant is free for the most part to choose in which court he wishes to commence his application because most of the orders available can be made by all three courts. However, this apparent freedom is curtailed in several ways and a clear understanding of the restrictions is needed before advice can sensibly be given about commencing an application in the family proceedings court, which is the court with which this book is concerned.

1.2 FAMILY PROCEEDINGS

By section 8(3) and (4) of the Act, for the purposes of the Act, 'family proceedings' means any proceedings:

(a) under the inherent jurisdiction of the High Court in relation to children; and

(b) any application made under:

  (i)   Parts I, II and IV of the Act

  (ii) the Matrimonial Causes Act 1973

(iii)   the Domestic Violence and Matrimonial Proceedings Act 1976

(iv)   the Adoption Act 1976

(v)   the Domestic Proceedings and Magistrates' Courts Act 1978

(vi)   sections 1 and 9 of the Matrimonial Homes Act 1983

(vii)   Part III of the Matrimonial and Family Proceedings Act 1984.

1.3   RESTRICTIONS ON VENUE

(a)   Subject to the exceptions discussed in chapter 2, a number of important applications must be commenced in the family proceedings court. They may be transferred to other courts in accordance with the criteria laid down in the Children (Allocation of Proceedings) Order 1991 (SI 1991 No. 1677), which is considered in chapter 3.

(b)   Secondly, where 'family proceedings' are already pending in another court you should not commence separate proceedings for a section 8 order (residence, contact, prohibited steps order or specific issue order). You should apply for your section 8 order in the proceedings already commenced.

(c)   Thirdly, the considerations which were relevant under the old jurisdictional system to the decision about where to commence proceedings (i.e., cost, speed of hearing etc.) will be equally pertinent under the new law where the choice is not determined by the first two restrictions considered above. It may well be that the legal aid authorities will insist that the proceedings are at least commenced in the cheapest venue.

1.4   EXAMPLES

A few examples will illustrate how the jurisdiction works:

(a)   A husband tells you that his wife has commenced proceedings in the county court for divorce and that she is applying for a residence order in respect of the children of the family in the divorce proceedings. Father does not object to his wife having a residence order, but he wishes to have more contact with the children than his wife is prepared to allow. The proper course is to make an application for a section 8 contact order in the divorce proceedings (which are of course 'family proceedings' – see above) and not to commence separate proceedings in any other court.

(b)   A father of an illegitimate son who wishes to have contact with his child tells you that his ex-girlfriend, the mother, will not let him see the little boy. He also tells you that the mother of the child has brought proceedings in the county court under the Domestic Violence and Matrimonial Proceedings Act (DVMPA) 1976 to oust him from the house in which they have been living together. He will of course be a respondent in those proceedings, so all he needs to do is to make an application in the DVMPA 1976 proceedings (which are 'family proceedings') for a section 8 contact order.

(c)   The father of an illegitimate child instructs you that the mother has made an application in the magistrates' court for financial provision under Schedule 1 to the Children Act 1989, but that she is unwilling to let him see the child. He wants to see the child but he does not wish to pay as much as the mother is demanding by way of maintenance. The appropriate course for the father is to respond in the proceedings already begun by the mother in the magistrates' court (which are 'family proceedings') and to apply for a section 8 contact order in the same proceedings.

1.5   SUMMARY

With every prospective application, first satisfy yourself about three matters:

(a)   Is the application one which by the Children (Allocation of Proceedings) Order 1991 *must* be commenced in the magistrates' court?

(b)   Are there other 'family proceedings' pending in another court in which you could obtain your order?

(c)   Where will proceedings be cheaper and quicker?

1.6   GENERAL PRINCIPLES

The welfare principle

Whenever a court determines any question with respect to the upbringing of a child or the administration of a child's property (or the application of any income from it), the court's *paramount consideration is the child's welfare* (section 1(1)).

This is not a change in the law because it was almost always the case that whenever any such question fell to be determined the first and paramount consideration was the welfare of the child. The words 'first and' do not add to the meaning of that phrase.

The delay principle

In any proceedings in which any question with respect to the upbringing of a child arises, the court *must* have regard to the general principle that any delay in determining the question is likely to prejudice the welfare of the child (section 1(2)).

Statutory checklist

Section 1(3) provides that the court shall have regard in particular to:

(a) *wishes and feelings* of the child, as far as they can be ascertained

(b) physical, emotional and educational *needs*

(c) likely effect of any *change*

(d) *age, sex, background* and any relevant *characteristics*

(e) any *harm* – past or future

(f) *capacity* of his parents or other relevant person to meet his needs

(g) range of *powers* available to the court.

Practitioners should become as familiar with section 1(3) of the Children Act 1989 as they are with section 25 of the Matrimonial Causes Act 1973.

Because the magistrates have to give reasons for their decision (see chapter 2) they are likely to frame their reasons around the checklist. It would be sensible for any advocate, therefore, to shape his or her submissions around the checklist too.

Although there is no mention of it in the statutory checklist, the argument that siblings should be kept together must still be relevant.

Checklist not exhaustive

Section 1(3) provides that 'a court shall have regard *in particular to* . . .', so the court is entitled to take into account other relevant matters.

Application of checklist

You should note, however, that the checklist applies only in contested section 8 proceedings and in proceedings under Part IV of the Act.

No order at all

The court must always ask itself this question:

Is the order better for the child than no order at all?

If the answer is no then the court should make no order (section 1(5)).

This is a new concept. To this extent the Act favours non-intervention. It has been said by Professor Stephen Cretney that the Children Act 1989 in some respects 'privatises' the family. Another way of looking at it is that all orders sought from the court will have to be justified. Practitioners will have to be prepared in particular to be able to justify the court's making a consent order. Section 1(5) creates a presumption *against* an order being made.

Opinions differ about this but it is likely that the court would take the view that an order is justified if, for example, housing is said to be dependent on the making of a residence order in favour of one party.

An applicant may also be able to argue that an order is needed because of benefit entitlement.

Chapter 2

Provisions Relevant to all Applications

2.1 VENUE

Subject to two important exceptions considered below, by article 3(1) of the Children (Allocation of Proceedings) Order 1991, proceedings under the following sections *must* be commenced in the magistrates' court:

(a) section 25 (secure accommodation)

(b) section 31 (care and supervision orders)

(c) section 33(7) (leave to change name of or remove from the United Kingdom child in care)

(d) section 34 (contact with a child in care)

(e) section 36 (education supervision orders)

(f) section 43 (child assessment orders)

(g) section 44 (emergency protection orders)

(h) section 45 (duration of emergency protection orders)

(i) section 46(7) (application by police officer for emergency protection order)

(j)   section 48 (powers to assist discovery of children)

(k)   section 50 (recovery orders)

(l)   section 75 (protection of children in an emergency)

(m)   section 77(6) (appeal against steps taken under section 77(1))

(n)   section 102 (powers of constable to assist etc).

(o)   paragraph 19 of Schedule 2 (approval of arrangements to assist child to live abroad)

(p)   paragraph 23 of Schedule 2 (contribution orders)

(q)   paragraph 8 of Schedule 8 (certain appeals)

(r)   section 21 of the Adoption Act 1976.

The exceptions are:

(a)   Proceedings of a kind mentioned in (b), (e), (f), (g), (i) or (j) above, and which arise out of an *investigation* directed by the High Court or a county court, *must* be commenced:

(i)   in the court which directs the investigation (where that court is the High Court or a care centre), or

(ii)   in such care centre as the court which directs the investigation may order (article 3(2)).

(b)   Proceedings of a kind mentioned in (a) to (k), (n) or (o) above *must* be made to the court in which are pending other proceedings, in respect of the same child, which are also of the kind mentioned (article 3(3)).

2.2   RESPONDENTS

In the case of each application those persons who are to be respondents are set out in column (iii) of Schedule 2 to the Family Proceedings Courts (Children Act 1989) Rules 1991 ('the Rules') on pages 214 to 217 (Rule 7(1)).

2.3 WRITTEN NOTICE

In every application the applicant is obliged to give *written notice* of proceedings, and of the date, time and place of the hearing or directions appointment fixed, to the persons set out in column (iv) of Schedule 2 to the Rules (Rule 4(3)).

2.4 FILING THE APPLICATION

With every application you must file (which means 'deposit with the justices' clerk' (Rule 1(2)) the application in respect of *each child* in the appropriate form in Schedule 1 to the Rules together with sufficient copies for one to be served on each respondent. If there is no prescribed form in Schedule 1 (unlikely), you can draft your own form; the only requirement is that it must be in writing (Rule 4(1)(a)).

2.5 ACTION BY JUSTICES' CLERK

In every case the justices' clerk on receipt of the documents filed *must* consider whether directions need to be given (see chapter 5).

He must then:

(a) fix the date, time and place for a hearing or a directions appointment, allowing sufficient time for the applicant to comply with the service rules (see below)

(b) endorse the date, time and place so fixed upon the copies of the application filed and

(c) return the copies to the applicant forthwith (Rule 4(2)).

2.6 SERVICE

Service on the respondent

If you know the respondent has a solicitor, service may be effected:

(a) by delivering the document to the solicitor's address for service

(b) by sending it by first-class post to the solicitor's address for service

(c)   via the document exchange

(d)   by sending a legible fax.

If you do not know that the respondent has a solicitor, service may be effected:

(a)   by personal delivery to the respondent

(b)   by delivering it to his residence or his last known residence

(c)   by sending it by first-class post to his residence or his last known residence (Rule 8(1)).

Unless the contrary is proved a document is deemed to have been served:

(a)   in the case of postal service, on the second business day after posting

(b)   in the case of service by DX, on the second business day after the day on which it is left at the DX (Rule 8(6)).

Service by child

Where a child is required to serve a document service must be by:

(a)   the solicitor acting for the child

(b)   where there is no solicitor, the guardian *ad litem*

(c)   where there is neither solicitor nor guardian, the justices' clerk (Rule 8(3)).

Service on a child

Subject to any direction by the clerk or the court, service of any document *on a child* must be effected by serving:

(a)   the solicitor acting for the child

(b)   where there is no such solicitor, the guardian *ad litem*

(c)   where there is neither a solicitor nor guardian, *and only with the leave* of the clerk or the court, the child himself (Rule 8(4)).

Statement of service

You must at or before the first directions appointment or hearing (whichever occurs first) file a statement that service of a copy of the application has been effected on each respondent and that written notice has been given as appropriate (see above). The statement should indicate the manner, date, time and place of service or, in the case of postal service, the date, time and place of posting (Rule 8(7)).

2.7 DOCUMENTARY EVIDENCE

You must file and serve on the parties, any welfare officer and any guardian *ad litem*, written statements of the substance of the oral evidence you intend to adduce at the hearing.

This is a very important innovation in the magistrates' court and should make the lower court a more attractive venue, since it will lessen the chances of being taken by surprise, and being forced to take hurried instructions in the corridor while the magistrates take an unscheduled coffee break.

Each statement must be *signed* and *dated* and must contain a *declaration* that the maker of the statement believes it to be true, and understands that it may be placed before the court.

You must also file and serve copies of any other documents, including experts' reports, upon which you intend to rely. Serve these by such time as the clerk or the court directs, or, if there is no direction, before the hearing or appointment.

If you do not comply with Rule 17 as to the filing of statements and documents, you will not be permitted to call your evidence unless you obtain leave to do so at the hearing (Rule 17(1)).

Supplementary statements may be served subject to any direction given by the clerk or the court about the timing of statements (Rule 17(2)).

Amendment of Documents

You need the leave of the clerk or the court to amend any document which has been filed or served. Leave must be requested in writing. On considering the request, the clerk or the court may:

(a)   grant the request or

(b) invite the parties or any of them to make representations (within a specified period) as to whether an order permitting amendment should be made (Rule 19).

Any amended document must be filed and served on all parties, and the amendments must be identified (Rule 19(3)).

2.8 ORAL EVIDENCE

The clerk or the court must keep a note of the substance of the oral evidence given at the hearing (and also of any oral evidence given at directions hearings) (Rule 20).

2.9 EXAMINATION OF CHILD

The child may not be medically or psychiatrically examined or otherwise assessed *without the leave of the court.* An application for leave should be served on all parties and on the guardian *ad litem,* unless the clerk or court directs otherwise (Rule 18(1) and (2)).

2.10 ATTENDANCE OF CHILD

If the child is a party to the proceedings he *may* attend. Proceedings may take place in the absence of the child or any other party, however, if:

(a) the court considers it in the interests of the child, having regard to the matters to be discussed or the evidence to be given, *and*

(b) the child is represented by a guardian *ad litem* or a solicitor (Rule 16(2)).

When considering the interests of the child in this context, the guardian, the child's solicitor and (if he is of sufficient understanding) the child himself, must be given an opportunity to make representations.

Part IV and Part V proceedings

Section 95 of the Act *permits* a court when considering whether or not to make an order under Part IV (care and supervision orders) or under Part V (orders for the protection of children) to *order* the child concerned to attend court at *any stage* of the proceedings.

2.11   ATTENDANCE OF OTHERS

Parties must attend directions appointments unless directed otherwise.

The court can exclude *any party* (including the child) from any part of the proceedings provided the conditions in Rule 16(2) above are met.

2.12   NON-ATTENDANCE

Failure by respondent to appear

If the court is satisfied that an absent respondent has received reasonable notice of the date of the hearing or that the circumstances of the case justify proceeding with the hearing, the court may begin to hear the application in the absence of the respondent (Rule 16(4)).

Failure by the applicant to attend

If one or more respondents appear, but the applicant does not, the court may refuse the application or, if sufficient evidence has previously been received, the court may proceed in the absence of the applicant (Rule 16(5)).

No party attends

The court may refuse the application (Rule 16(6)).

2.13   EVIDENCE OF CHILD

Where a child who is called as a witness does not, in the opinion of the court, understand the nature of an oath, his evidence may be heard by the court if, in its opinion:

    (a)   the child understands that it his duty to speak the truth and

    (b)   he has sufficient understanding to justify his evidence being heard (section 96 of the Act).

See also the Children (Admissibility of Hearsay Evidence) Order 1990. This order permits courts to receive hearsay evidence in cases connected with the upbringing, maintenance or welfare of children.

2.14 CAN THE MAGISTRATES SEE THE CHILD?

Magistrates cannot see the child.

2.15 WELFARE REPORTS

A court considering any question with respect to a child under the Act may ask:

(a)   a probation officer or

(b)   the local authority to arrange for one of its officers or such other person as the authority considers appropriate,

to report to the court on matters relating to the welfare of the child (section 7).

The report may be made in writing or given orally, as required by the court. The welfare officer *must* file any written report by such time as the clerk or the court directs or, in the absence of any directions, *at least five days before the hearing*. The clerk must, as soon as practicable, *serve* a copy of the report on the parties and on the guardian (Rule 13(2)).

The welfare officer *must* attend the hearing (unless excused by the court or the clerk) if the clerk gives him notice that his report will be given or considered at that hearing (Rule 13(1)).

Any party may question the welfare officer about his report at the hearing.

2.16 READING THE DOCUMENTS

Before the hearing, the justice or justices who will be dealing with the case must read any documents which have been filed (Rule 21(1)).

2.17 'BATTING ORDER'

The clerk may give directions as to the order of speeches and evidence.

Subject to any such directions, the parties and the guardian *ad litem* must adduce their evidence in the following order:

(a)   the applicant

(b)   any party with parental responsibility for the child

(c)   other respondents

(d)   the guardian *ad litem*

(e)   the child, if he is a party and there is no guardian *ad litem* (Rule 21(2) and (3)).

2.18   WITHDRAWAL OF APPLICATION

An application may only be withdrawn with the leave of the court. You must serve a written request for leave, setting out the reasons for the request. However, if all parties and, if appointed, the guardian *ad litem*, are present, the request may be made orally (Rule 5(1), (2) and (3)).

The request *must* be granted if:

(a)   the parties consent in writing

(b)   the guardian (if any) has had an opportunity to make representations and

(c)   the court thinks fit (Rule 5(4)(a)).

Otherwise, a date must be fixed for the hearing of the request (Rule 5(4)(b)).

2.19   RECORD BEFORE THE ORDER

Before the court makes an order or refuses an application or request, the clerk must record in writing:

(a)   the names of the justices constituting the relevant court and

(b)   (in consultation with the justice or justices) the reason for the court's decision and any finding of fact (Rule 21(5)).

2.20   REASONS

When making an order, or refusing an application, the court must state any findings of fact and the reasons for the court's decision (Rule 21(6)).

2.21 FORM OF THE ORDER

When the court announces its decision the clerk must, as soon as practicable, make a record of any order in the appropriate form in Schedule 1 to the Rules. If there is no prescribed form, the order is simply required to be in writing (Rule 21(7)(a)).

2.22 SERVICE OF ORDER

The clerk is obliged, as soon as practicable, to serve a copy of the order on the parties to the proceedings and on any person with whom the child is living (Rule 21(7)(b)).

In respect of:

(a) a section 48(4) order

(b) an *ex parte*:

   (i) prohibited steps order,

   (ii) specific issue order or

   (iii) order under section 44, 48(9), 50, 75(1) or 102(1) of the Act,

the *applicant* must serve a copy of the order in the appropriate form (in Schedule 1 to the Rules) *within 48 hours* after the making of the order on:

(a) each party

(b) any person who has actual care of the child, or v/ho had such care immediately prior to the making of the order

(c) in the case of an order under section 44, 48(9), 50, 75(1) or 102(1), the local authority in whose area the child lives or is found (Rule 21(8)).

2.23 EXTENSION, VARIATION AND DISCHARGE

In respect of any such application, the respondents include the parties to the proceedings leading to the order which it is sought to have extended, varied or discharged (Schedule 2 to the Rules).

There is a general form for an application to vary or discharge an order or direction under section 10(6), section 4(9), section 38(8)(b) or section 43(12) (CHA 55 to be found on pages 196–200 of the Rules).

There are prescribed forms for applications to extend, vary or discharge orders made under other sections of the Act: see Schedule 1 to the Rules.

2.24 COSTS

The court may, *at any time,* order a party to pay the whole or part of any other party's costs. A party against whom the court is considering making a costs order must be given an opportunity to make representations as to why an order should not be made (Rule 22).

Beware the court's power to make a 'wasted costs order' against a legal or other representative under the Magistrates' Courts (Costs against Legal Representatives in Civil Proceedings) Rules 1991 (SI 1991 No. 2096).

2.25 TIME

If a period of time, being seven days or less, would include a 'non-business day', that day shall be excluded (Rule 15(2)).

Where the time fixed for filing a document expires on a day when the clerk's office is closed, the document will be filed in time if it is filed on the next day on which the office is open (Rule 15(3)).

If the Rules prescribe a period of time within which or by which an act is to be performed, that period cannot be extended save by a direction of the clerk or the court (Rule 15(4)).

2.26 PRIVACY

If the court considers it expedient in the interests of the child, it may hear proceedings in private (Rule 16(7)).

2.27 CONFIDENTIALITY

Documents held by the court (other than records of orders) *cannot* be disclosed to anyone except the parties, their legal representatives, the guardian *ad litem,* the Legal Aid Board or a welfare officer *without leave* of the clerk of the court (Rule 23).

2.28 SOLICITOR FOR THE CHILD

By Rule 12(1), a solicitor appointed for the child shall represent him:

(a) in accordance with instructions received from the guardian *ad litem* (unless the solicitor considers, having taken into account the guardian's view and any direction of the court, that the child wishes to give instructions which conflict with those of the guardian and that he is able, having regard to his understanding to give instructions on his own behalf, in which case the solicitor shall conduct the proceedings in accordance with instructions received from the child) or

(b) when no guardian *ad litem* has been appointed and the child has sufficient understanding to instruct a solicitor and wishes to do so, in accordance with instructions received from the child or

(c) in default of instructions under the above paragraphs, in furtherance of the best interests of the child.

Termination of appointment

Both the child and the guardian may apply to the court for an order terminating the appointment of the solicitor. The solicitor and, where applicable, the guardian and, if he is of sufficient understanding, the child himself must be given an opportunity to make representations (Rule 12(3) and (4)).

2.29 'SUFFICIENT UNDERSTANDING'

Assistance may be derived from *Gillick* v *West Norfolk and Wisbech Area Health Authority* [1986] AC 112.

2.30 PUBLICITY

By section 97(2), no person may publish any material (including any picture or representation) which is intended, or likely, to identify:

(a) any child as being involved in any proceedings before a magistrates' court

(b) an address or school as being that of a child involved in any proceedings.

Chapter 3

Transfer of Proceedings

The provisions are set out in the Children (Allocation of Proceedings) Order 1991 (SI 1991 No. 1677).

3.1 TRANSFER FROM ONE MAGISTRATES' COURT TO ANOTHER

By article 6 of the Children (Allocation of Proceedings) Order 1991, a magistrates' court ('the transferring court') *must* transfer proceedings under the Act or under the Adoption Act 1976 to another magistrates' court ('the receiving court') where:

(a)   having regard to the general principle that any delay in determining any question relating to the upbringing of a child is likely to prejudice the welfare of a child ('the section 1(2) principle') the transferring court considers the transfer is in the interests of the child:

(i)   because it is likely *significantly* to accelerate the determination of the proceedings,

(ii)   because it would be appropriate for those proceedings to be heard together with other family proceedings pending in the receiving court, or

(iii)   for some other reason

and

(b)   the receiving court, by its justices' clerk, consents to the transfer.

3.2 TRANSFER FROM MAGISTRATES' COURT TO COUNTY COURT *BY* MAGISTRATES' COURT

Proceedings which *may* be transferred

Subject to certain restrictions, the magistrates' court *may*, upon application by a party or of its own motion, transfer to a county court certain proceedings, namely, those in respect of:

(a)   secure accommodation (section 25)

(b)   care and supervision orders (section 31)

(c)   leave to change name of or to remove from the UK a child in care (section 33(7))

(d)   parental contact (section 34)

(e)   education supervision orders (section 36)

(f)   child assessment orders (section 43)

(g)   recovery orders (section 50)

(h)   power of constable to assist (section 102)

(i)   approval of arrangements to assist a child to live abroad (paragraph 19 of Schedule 2)

(j)   section 21 of the Adoption Act 1976 (as amended by the Act).

Criteria

By article 7(1) of the Children (Allocation of Proceedings) Order 1991, the court must consider whether it is in the interests of the child to transfer, having regard to the section 1(2) principle and the following questions:

(a)   whether the proceedings are exceptionally grave, important or complex, in particular:

(i)   because of complicated or conflicting evidence about the risks involved to the child's physical or moral well-being or about other matters relating to the welfare of the child

    (ii)   because of the number of parties

    (iii)   because of a conflict of law with another jurisdiction

    (iv)   because of some novel and difficult point of law, or

    (v)   because of some question of general public interest

  (b)   whether it would be appropriate for those proceedings to be heard together with other family proceedings which are pending in another court and

  (c)   whether transfer is likely significantly to accelerate the determination of the proceedings where:

    (i)   no other method of doing so, including transfer to another magistrates' court is appropriate and

    (ii)   delay would *seriously prejudice* the interests of the child.

Restrictions

Proceedings relating to secure accommodation (section 25) and powers of a constable to assist (section 102) may *only* be transferred to a county court in order to be heard together with other family proceedings which arise out of the same circumstances as gave rise to the proceedings to be transferred and which are pending in another court (article 7(3)).

Secure accommodation proceedings may not be transferred from a magistrates' court which is *not* a family proceedings court.

Proceedings under the Act or under the Adoption Act 1976 to which article 7 does not apply

A magistrates' court may transfer the proceedings to a county court where, having regard to the section 1(2) principle, it considers that in the interests of the child the proceedings can be dealt with *more appropriately* in that county court.

Refusal by magistrates' court to transfer proceedings

By article 9 of the Children (Allocation of Proceedings) Order 1991, if the magistrates' court refuses to transfer proceedings under article 7, a party to the proceedings may apply to the *care centre* for the petty sessions or London commission area in which the magistrates' court is situated.

Upon hearing the application the court may:

(a)   transfer the proceedings to itself where, having regard to the section 1(2) principle and the questions set out in article 7(1)(a) to (c) (see criteria, above), it considers it to be in the interests of the child to do so, *or*

(b)   transfer the proceedings to the High Court if, having regard to the section 1(2) principle, it considers:

(i)   that the proceedings are appropriate for determination in the High Court, and

(ii)   that such determination would be in the interests of the child.

Article 7(1) criteria cease to apply

A county court may transfer proceedings back to the magistrates' court before trial where, having regard to the section 1(2) principle and the interests of the child, the county court considers that the article 7(1) criteria cited by the magistrates' court as the reason for transfer no longer apply (article 11).

3.3   ALLOCATION OF PROCEEDINGS TO COUNTY COURTS

Proceedings under Part I or Part II of or Schedule 1 to the Act

Where an application is to be transferred from a magistrates' court to a county court, it must be transferred to a divorce county court *unless* (save for a section 8 application) it is to be transferred to a county court in order to be consolidated with other proceedings, in which case it must be transferred to the county court in which those other proceedings are pending (article 15).

A section 8 application may be transferred to a county court which is not a family hearing centre but, if the proceedings are opposed, the county court must transfer the matter for trial to a family hearing centre.

Proceedings under the Adoption Act 1976

Where proceedings under the Adoption Act 1976 are to be transferred from the magistrates' court to a county court, they must be transferred to a divorce county court (article 17(2)).

Proceedings under Part III, Part IV or Part V of the Act

Where an application under Part III, IV or V of the Act is to be transferred from the magistrates' court to the county court, it must be transferred to the care centre for the petty sessions area or London commission area in which the magistrates' court is situated (article 18(3)).

Chapter 4

Directions

4.1 INTRODUCTION

Those who practise in the county courts and in the Family Division of the High Court will be familiar with the use of the directions appointment as a means whereby those courts control the progress of proceedings. The power of both the justices' clerk and magistrates to give directions is a cornerstone of the procedure under the new Act and an important innovation in the magistrates' court. The Family Proceedings Courts (Children Act 1989) Rules 1991 ('the Rules') apply.

4.2 THE JUSTICES' CLERK

When the clerk receives any application, or where proceedings have been transferred to his court, he *must consider* whether directions for the conduct of the proceedings need to be given (Rule 14(2)).

Such directions may deal with:

(a) the timetable for the proceedings

(b) variation of the time within which or by which an act is required to be done

(c) the attendance of the child

(d) the appointment of a guardian *ad litem* or solicitor for the child

(e)   the service of documents

(f)   the submission of evidence *including experts' reports*

(g)   the preparation of welfare reports

(h)   the transfer of the proceedings to another court

(i)   consolidation with other proceedings

(j)   the order of evidence and speeches at the final hearing.

By Rule 4(2) the clerk is obliged, when he receives an application, to fix the date, time and place for a directions appointment or a hearing. Remember that the applicant must serve each respondent with a copy of the application endorsed with those details.

4.3   THE DIRECTIONS APPOINTMENT

A directions appointment may be held by a justices' clerk or a single justice. Before the appointment each party should consider directions he wishes the court to make, for example, whether the application should stay in the magistrates' court or be dealt with by a higher court.

Directions may be given, varied or revoked either:

(a)   of the clerk or the court's own motion, in which case the parties (including the guardian *ad litem* and, where the direction involves a welfare report, the welfare officer) must be given notice and the opportunity to attend or to make written representations, *or*

(b)   on the written request of a party, specifying the directions sought. The request must be filed and served on the other parties and the clerk must fix a date for the hearing of the request and give the parties not less than two days' notice: Rule 14(7) *or*

(c)   on a similar written request, to which the other parties *consent* and which they have signed (Rule 14(5)). The clerk or the court must either grant the request or fix a hearing date, giving the parties not less than two days' notice.

All parties *must attend* a directions appointment of which they have been given notice unless the clerk or the court directs otherwise (Rule 16(1)). (For parties see above.)

4.4 URGENT CASES

In cases of urgency, Rule 14(6) provides that a party may apply for directions:

(a)   orally (with or without notice to any other party), *or*

(b)   in writing (with or without notice to any other party).

4.5 SPECIAL DIRECTIONS

A party may use the written request for directions procedure set out above to seek an *interim* section 8 order or an *interim* care or supervision order. However, such orders may only be made if:

(a)   a written request for the order has been made and signed by all the parties

(b)   the court has already made one such order

(c)   the terms of the order sought are exactly the same as the last order made (Rule 28).

This rule provides in effect a 'repeat prescription' for interim consent section 8 and care or supervision orders.

Chapter 5

Applying for Leave

5.1 INTRODUCTION

As we see in more detail later, certain categories of persons may apply to the family proceedings court as of right, whereas others must obtain the leave of the court before applying for orders. Whenever a person needs to apply for leave the procedure described in this chapter should be followed.

5.2 MAKING THE APPLICATION

As usual the procedure is governed by the Family Proceedings Courts (Children Act 1989) Rules 1991 ('the Rules'). Rule 3 provides that a person seeking leave must file:

(a) a *written* request for leave, setting out the reasons for the application and

(b) a *draft* of the application for the making of which leave is sought. The draft application must be in the appropriate form in Schedule 1 to the Rules. (If there is no prescribed form, file a written draft.)

For example, if you need leave to apply for a section 8 residence order you should fill in a draft CHA 10 (to be found on pages 43 to 50 of the Rules), and you must write out a request for leave, giving your reasons for making the application. There is at present no prescribed form for the written request.

Filing the draft application and request

You must deposit the relevant documents with the justices' clerk, remembering to file enough copies for each proposed respondent.

The court's powers

The court (which may be a single magistrate) may on considering the request for leave *either*:

(a)   grant leave, *or*

(b)   direct that a date be fixed for the hearing of the request.

If the court adopts the latter course the clerk must fix a date and give notice to the applicant and to such other persons as the court requires to be notified of the date (Rule 3(2)).

It appears, therefore, that the court may grant leave *ex parte*, that is without informing anyone of the request for leave.

The criteria

(a)   Applying for leave to make an application for a section 8 order:

(i)   *The child as applicant.* The court may only grant leave if satisfied that he has sufficient understanding to make the proposed application (section 10(8)).

(ii)   *Other applicants.* In deciding whether or not to grant leave the court must have particular regard to:

(1)   the nature of the proposed application

(2)   the applicant's connection with the child

(3)   any risk there might be of the proposed application's disrupting the child's life to such an extent that he would be harmed by it and

(4)   where the child is being looked after by a local authority, the authority's plans for the child's future and the wishes and feelings of the child's parents (section 10(9)).

(b)   If the applicant is seeking leave to make any other application (e.g., contact with a child in care under section 34), it is likely that similar criteria will be applied.

Foster parent as applicant

A person who is, or was at any time within the last six months, a local authority foster parent of a child, *may not* apply for leave to apply for a section 8 order *unless*:

(a)   he has the consent of the authority, *or*

(b)   he is a relative of the child, *or*

(c)   the child has lived with him for at least three years preceding the application (section 9(3)).

5.3   LEAVE GRANTED

When leave is granted, you proceed with your application in the usual way, in accordance with Rule 4 (except that you do not need to file the application because this will already have been done).

Chapter 6

Guardian *ad litem*

6.1 INTRODUCTION

Those who have experience of pre-Act care proceedings in the magistrates' court will be familiar with the role played by guardians *ad litem*. Under the Act, there is a presumption in favour of the appointment of a guardian *ad litem* in a wide range of proceedings. The function of the guardian is to represent the child's interests in court. Guardians are usually highly experienced social workers.

6.2 THE APPOINTMENT

In any *specified proceedings* the court *must* appoint a guardian *ad litem* for the child concerned *unless* satisfied that it is not necessary to do so in order to safeguard the child's interests (section 41(1) of the Act and Rule 10(1)).

Specified proceedings are proceedings:

(a) for a care or supervision order

(b) in which the court has given a direction under section 37(1) and has made, or is considering whether to make, an interim care order

(c) for the discharge of a care order or the variation or discharge of a supervision order

(d) under section 39(4) (substitution of supervision order for care order)

(e)   in which the court is considering whether to make a residence order with respect to a child who is the subject of a care order

(f)   with respect to contact between a child who is the subject of a care order and any other person

(g)   under Part V (including child assessment order, EPO and child recovery order)

(h)   on an appeal against:

(i)   the making of, or refusal to make, a care order, supervision order or any section 34 order

(ii)   the making of, or refusal to make, a residence order with respect to a child who is the subject of a care order

(iii)   the variation or discharge, or refusal of an application to vary or discharge, the type of order mentioned in (i) or (ii)

(iv)   the refusal of an application under section 39(4) or

(v)   the making of, or refusal to make, an order under Part V (orders for the protection of children) (section 41(6)).

Rule 2(2) of the Family Proceedings Courts (Children Act 1989) Rules 1991 ('the Rules') adds:

(i)   proceedings under section 25 (secure accommodation)

(j)   applications under section 33(7) (leave to change surname of a child in care or remove him from the UK)

(k)   proceedings under paragraph 19(1) of Schedule 2 (leave for local authority to arrange for a child in their care to live abroad)

(l)   applications under paragraph 6(3) of Schedule 3 (extension of supervision orders).

In specified proceedings a guardian may be appointed at any stage either by the court or on the application of any party, whatever the decision at the commencement of the proceedings (Rule 10(2), (3) and (4)).

6.3 POWERS AND DUTIES OF A GUARDIAN *AD LITEM*

The starting-point

The guardian is under a duty to safeguard the interests of the child in the manner prescribed by the Rules (section 41(2)(b)). Rule 11(1) provides that he must have regard to:

(a) the 'delay principle' (section 1(2))

(b) the statutory checklist (except for section 1(3)(g) – the range of powers available to the court).

Basic duties

He must:

(a) advise the child (such advice will vary with the age and understanding of the child)

(b) appoint and instruct a solicitor to represent the child (Rule 11(2))

(If the child already has a solicitor, or intends to conduct the proceedings without one, the guardian must tell the justices' clerk, who thereafter may give directions as to the guardian's duties and the part he is to play in the proceedings. The clerk or the court may also permit the guardian himself to have legal representation in those circumstances.)

(c) notify any person whom he thinks should be joined as a party in order to safeguard the interests of the child of his right to apply to be joined (Rule 11(6)).

Attendance at court

The guardian *must* (unless excused by the clerk or the court) *attend* all directions appointments and hearings and must advise the clerk or the court on:

(a) whether the child is of sufficient understanding for any purpose (including the child's refusal to submit to an examination or other assessment)

(b) the wishes of the child (including his attendance at court)

(c) the forum for and timing of the proceedings

(d)   options available to the court and the suitability of each option

(e)   any other relevant matter (Rule 11(4)).

If not given in writing, the guardian's advice must be recorded by the clerk or the court (Rule 11(5)).

Guardian's report

Subject to directions the guardian must file a *written* report advising on the interests of the child not less than *seven* days before the final hearing (Rule 11(7)).

Service

The guardian must serve and accept service of documents on behalf of the child. Where the child himself has not been served, and has sufficient understanding, the guardian should advise the child of the contents of any such documents (Rule 11(8)).

Investigations

The guardian must carry out such investigations as are necessary for him to discharge his duties, including:

(a)   interviewing as appropriate or as directed

(b)   bringing to the attention of the court such local authority records as he thinks relevant and

(c)   obtaining such professional assistance as he considers appropriate or as directed by the court (Rule 11(9)).

6.4   ACCESS TO LOCAL AUTHORITY RECORDS

A guardian *ad litem* may at all reasonable times *examine and take copies of*:

(a)   any records of, or held by, a local authority which were compiled in connection with the making, or proposed making, by any person of any application under the Act with respect to the child, or

(b)   any other records of, or held by, a local authority which were compiled in connection with any functions which stand referred to their social services committee under the Local Authority Social Services Act 1970, so far as those records relate to the child (section 42(1)).

6.5   ADMISSIBILITY OF COPY RECORDS

Where a guardian *ad litem* takes a copy of any record which he is entitled to examine, that copy (or any part of it) *shall be admissible* as evidence of any matter referred to in any report which he makes to the court or evidence which he gives in the proceedings (section 42(4)).

The provisions as to admissibility apply regardless of any enactment or rule of law which would otherwise prevent the record being admissible in evidence (section 42(3)).

6.6   APPOINTMENT OF SOLICITOR TO ACT FOR THE CHILD

Where a child is not represented by a solicitor *and*

(a)   no guardian *ad litem* has been appointed for the child and

(b)   the child has sufficient understanding to instruct a solicitor and wishes to do so and

(c)   it appears to the court that it would be in the best interests of the child for him to be represented by a solicitor,

the court may appoint a solicitor to act for the child (section 41(3) and (4)).

6.7   DURATION

The guardian must act for as long as the appointment directs unless the appointment is terminated earlier by the court (Rule 10(9)). If the court terminates the appointment it must give written reasons for doing so (Rule 10(10)).

Chapter 7

Applications for a Parental Responsibility Order

7.1 INTRODUCTION

Parental responsibility is the sum of lawful 'rights, duties, powers, responsibilities and authority' of a parent (section 3(1)).

It has been suggested that this includes the following rights:

(a) the right to physical possession of the child as against others

(b) the right to decide upon a child's education

(c) the right to consent to medical treatment

(d) the right to discipline the child

(e) the right to decide the child's religion

(f) the right to give consent to the child's marriage

(g) the right to have contact with the child.

The father of an illegitimate child may, therefore, wish to acquire parental responsibility for many reasons but specifically under the Act, if he does not have parental responsibility he would not be entitled to remove a child from accommodation provided under section 20 by the local authority because that right to remove (given by section 20(8)) is conferred only on 'a person who has parental responsibility'.

Further, his agreement would not be required to the child's adoption.

7.2 PRELIMINARIES

Is an application necessary?

(a)   Are the parties married?

If they are, there is no need to apply because *each* parent will have parental responsibility for the child (section 2(1)).

(b)   Have the parties, although unmarried at the time of the child's birth, subsequently entered into a 'parental responsibility agreement' under section 4(1)(b)?

If they have, make sure that it is in the form prescribed by regulations made by the Lord Chancellor in the Parental Responsibility Agreement Regulations 1991 (SI 1991 No. 1478). See CHA1* at the end of this chapter. If it is, then there is no need to apply for an order.

(c)   Does the father have a residence order in his favour?

If yes then there is no need to apply because if the court has made a residence order in his favour it will have made a parental responsibility order at the same time (section 12(1)).

(d)   Father appointed as guardian

If the father has been appointed as the child's guardian under section 5 of the Act then he will already have acquired parental responsibility.

(e)   Summary

So it is only in default of:

(i)   marriage

(ii)   a parental responsibility agreement

(iii)   a residence order in his favour, or

(iv)   his appointment as guardian

that the father of an illegitimate child who wishes to have parental responsibility for his child will need to apply to the court for an order.

Mother of an illegitimate child as applicant?

Section 4(1)(a) makes it clear that *only the father* may apply ('on the application of the father').

However, the father of an illegitimate child should not think that by not applying for an order for parental responsibility he can avoid liability to maintain his child. Section 3(4) specifically provides that:

> The fact that a person has, or does not have, parental responsibility for a child shall not affect—

> (a)   any obligation which he may have in relation to the child (such as a statutory duty to maintain the child).

On the other hand, even without parental responsibility, the father of an illegitimate child is still a parent under the Act and thus has the same right as any other parent to apply to the courts for any section 8 order (see section 10(4)), and under section 34(1) he is entitled to reasonable contact with any child of his in care.

All the above matters will have to be discussed with the applicant to establish whether an application is necessary and, assuming that it is, that you have sufficient instructions to fill out the form which will commence the application (see below).

Venue

As usual, ascertain whether any other family proceedings are pending in another court, in which case it may be possible to attach to them. If not, it is very likely that in most cases it will be appropriate to commence the application in the family proceedings court. There is, however, no obligation to do so.

The magistrates' court may transfer the application to a county court under the provisions set out in article 7 of the Children (Allocation of Proceedings) Order 1991 (SI 1991 No. 1677) – see chapter 3.

Leave

Not required if the applicant is the father.

7.3 MAKING THE APPLICATION

As with all applications in the magistrates' court, the Family Proceedings Courts (Children Act 1989) Rules 1991 ('the Rules') apply. The procedure you should follow is set out in chapter 2 of this book.

Filling in the form

Fill in Form CHA 1 which you will find on pages 20 to 23 of the Rules.

The form contains five sections. Like all the forms under the Act it is mostly self-explanatory and designed in such a way that as much information about the application as possible is conveyed in the form itself to the court and to all parties concerned. (For an example of a completed CHA 1 see end of this chapter.)

In the case of an application for parental responsibility you must serve the application at least *14 days* before the hearing (see column (ii) of Schedule 2 to the Rules on page 214 of the Rules).

Respondents

The following are respondents and must be served:

(a)   every person whom you believe to have parental responsibility for the child (in most applications by the father of an illegitimate child this will be the mother only)

(b)   if the child is the subject of a care order, every person whom you believe had parental responsibility prior to the making of the care order.

Giving notice

Look at column (iv) of Schedule 2 to the Rules, on pages 214 and 215.

The persons entitled to written notice of an application for an order for parental responsibility are:

(a)   every person caring for the child when the application is commenced

(b)   if applicable, the local authority providing accommodation for the child

(c)   if applicable, in the case of proceedings brought in respect of a child who is alleged to be staying in a certificated refuge, the person who is providing the refuge.

7.4   DIRECTIONS

See chapter 4.

7.5   THE ORDER

The parental responsibility order is made in form CHA 2 – page 24 of the Rules.

7.6   DURATION

A parental responsibility order can only end:

(a)   when the child reaches his 18th birthday

(b)   by order of the court made on the application of any person who has parental responsibility or, with leave of the court, the child himself (section 4(3)). The court may only grant leave if it is satisfied that the child has sufficient understanding to make the proposed application (section 4(4)).

O
Y
E
Z

CHA1*
Parental Responsibility Agreement

Section 4(1)(b)   The Children Act 1989

Date Recorded

◆ Please use black ink.

◆ The making of this agreement will **seriously** affect the legal position of both parents. You should both seek legal **advice before** completing this form.

◆ If there is more than one child, **you should** fill in a separate form for each child.

━━━━━━━━━ THE ━━ CHILDREN ━━ ACT ━━━━

This is a parental responsibility agreement between

the child's mother	Name *ALICE BROWN*
and	Address *6, NARFORD ROAD* *NEWTOWN, WESSEX*

the child's father	Name *ANDREW HARDY*
	Address *48 MOUNTVIEW ROAD* *BARCHESTER, WESSEX*

We agree that the father of the child named below should have parental responsibility for [him] [her] in addition to the mother.

Name	Boy/Girl	Date of birth	Date of 18th birthday
THOMAS HARDY	*BOY*	*19.7.1988*	*19.7.2006*

Ending of the agreement

Once a parental responsibility agreement has been made it can only end:

● by an order of the Court made on application of any person who has parental responsibility for the child.

● by an order of the Court made on the application of the child with leave of the Court.

● when the child reaches the age of 18.

Signed (mother)	*A. Brown*	Date	*27/11/1991*
Signature of witness	*B. Mount*	Date	*27/11/1991*
Signed (father)	*a. Hardy*	Date	*27/11/1991*
Signature of witness	*J. Townsend*	Date	*27/11/1991*

This agreement will not take effect until this form has been filed with the Principal Registry of the Family Division. Once this form has been completed and signed please take or send it and two copies to:

> The Principal Registry of the Family Division
> Somerset House
> Strand
> London WC2R 1LP

━━━━━━━━ THE ━━ CHILDREN ━━ ACT ━━━━

O
Y **CHA 1**
E
Z # Application for a Parental Responsibility Order

Section 4 (1) (a) The Children Act 1989   Date received by court

◆ Please use black ink.

◆ The notes on page 3 tell you what to do when you have completed the form.

◆ If there is more than one child you must fill in a separate form for each child.

◆ Only the father of the child can make this application.

◆ You should seek legal advice on the implications of acquiring parental responsibility before completing this form.

◆ If you have any concerns about giving your address or that of the child or any other address requested in this form, you may give an alternative address where papers can be served. However you must notify the court of the actual address on a separate form available from the court.

━━━━ THE ━━━━ CHILDREN ━━━━ ACT ━━━━

I apply to The *Barchester*   [High] [County] [Magistrates'] Court

                                              Case No.

for a Parental Responsibility Order

━━━━ THE ━━━━ CHILDREN ━━━━ ACT ━━━━

1 About the child

(a) The name of the child is
    Put the surname last.   *THOMAS HARDY*

(b) The child is a   ✓ boy   ☐ girl

(c) The child was born on   day   month   year
    the   *19*   *JULY*   *1988*   Age now *3*

(d) The child is at   *6, Narford Road*
    See note on addresses   *Newtown*
    at the top of this form.   *Wessex*

(e) The child lives with   ✓ the child's   ☐ the child's
    If the child does not live with   mother   father
    a parent please give the
    name of the person who is
    responsible for the child.

━━━━ THE ━━━━ CHILDREN ━━━━ ACT ━━━━

2 About the applicant

(a) My full name is
    Put the surname last.   *ANDREW HARDY*

(b) My title is   ✓ Mr   ☐ Other (say here)

(c) My full address is   *48 Mountview Road*
    See note on addresses   *Barchester, Wessex*
    at the top of this form.

(d) My telephone number is   Tel. *0931 455678*

(e) My solicitor is   Name *Davies Morgan & Co*
                             Address *18 High Street*
                                     Barchester, Wessex
                             Tel. *0931 766782* Fax *0931 766792* Ref *JVR*

━━━━ THE ━━━━ CHILDREN ━━━━ ACT ━━━━

1

3 Parental responsibility

Some other people may have "parental responsibility" for a child
The law says what "parental responsibility" is
and which people have it. These people include:

A the mother

B the father
if he was married to the child's mother
when the child was born

C the father
if he was **not** married to the child's mother
when the child was born
but he now has a residence order

or he now has a court order
which gives him parental responsibility

or he now has a formal "parental
responsibility agreement" with
the mother

or he has since married the mother

D a guardian of the child

E someone who holds a custody or residence order

F a local authority which has a care order

G someone who holds an emergency protection order

H any man or woman who has adopted the child

	Name	Address
I believe the people who have parental responsibility for this child are *See note on addresses at the top of page 1.*	ALICE BROWN	6, Norford Road Newtown, Wessex

━━━━ THE ━━━ CHILDREN ━━━ ACT ━━━━

4 About this application

(a) I am making this application because

The mother of the child and I have cohabited for the last five years. We have never married because she has always maintained that she was unwilling to give up her own residence and share my home.
Because of constant quarrels over that issue, we finally separated about five weeks ago. A week ago Miss Brown told me that she was intending to join a fanatical religious

                    continue on next page if necessary

4   About this application (continued)

(a) I am making this application because (continued)

> sect called the Zealots of the Rising Sun, and to ensure that Thomas will be brought up in their faith. I wish to ensure that I continue to have a say in my son's upbringing.

(b) The respondents will be   ● all those with parental responsibility, see part 3 above
                                        ● other people allowed by Rules of Court

(i) *You need not repeat the details of those respondents whose names and addresses have been given in part 3.*

(ii) *Please put the address where the respondent usually lives or where papers can be served. See note on addresses at the top of page 1.*

(iii) *You will have to serve a copy of this application on each of the respondents.*

The name of the respondent(s)	The respondent's address

THE ▬▬ CHILDREN ▬▬ ACT

5   Declaration

I declare that the information I have given is correct and complete to the best of my knowledge.

Signed   *a. Hardy*   Date   *16th October 1991*

THE ▬▬ CHILDREN ▬▬ ACT

What you (the person applying) must do next

♦ There is a Notice of Hearing on page 4. Fill in the boxes on the Notice.

♦ Take or send this form, Notice of Hearing and any supporting documentation to the court with enough copies for each respondent to be served. The top copy will be kept by the court and the other copies given or sent back to you for service.

♦ You **must** then serve the copies of the Application, the Notice of Hearing and any supporting documentation according to the Rules. You may also be required under the Rules to give notice of the proceedings to other people.

THE ▬▬ CHILDREN ▬▬ ACT

In the   [High] [County] [Magistrates'] Court

at

(When writing to the Court please state the Case No.)   **Case No.**

Tel.   Fax

THE ■ CHILDREN ■ ACT

Notice of a [Hearing] [Directions Appointment]

You are named as a Respondent in these proceedings

about the child   *Thomas Hardy*

☑ a boy   ☐ a girl

born on the   *19 July 1988*

You must read this Notice now

THE ■ CHILDREN ■ ACT

About the [Hearing] [Directions Appointment]

name of applicant

ANDREW HARDY

has made an application to the Court.

The Court has been asked to make a parental responsibility order.

THE ■ CHILDREN ■ ACT

To be completed by the Court

The Court will hear this at

on

at   o'clock

the time allowed is

THE ■ CHILDREN ■ ACT

WHAT YOU MUST DO

♦ There is a copy of the application with this Notice of Hearing. Read the application now. You do not have to fill in any part.

♦ You should obtain legal advice from a solicitor or, alternatively, from an advice agency. The Law Society administers a national panel of solicitors to represent children and other parties involved in proceedings relating to children. Addresses of solicitors (including panel members) and advice agencies can be obtained from the Yellow Pages and the Solicitors Regional Directory which can be found at Citizens Advice Bureaux, Law Centres and any local library. A solicitor or advice agency will also be able to advise you as to whether you will be eligible for legal aid.

date

4

OYEZ The Solicitors' Law Stationery Society Ltd , Oyez House. 7 Spa Road. London SE 16 3QQ   8 91 F20632

CHA 1   5037501

* * * * *

Chapter 8

Applications for Section 8 Orders

8.1 INTRODUCTION

Residence order

Under the new legislation the courts can no longer make orders awarding custody and access in relation to children, whether legitimate or illegitimate. The old custody order has been replaced by a 'residence order'. This order (and the three other orders considered below) is called a 'Section 8 order', so called because it is defined in section 8 of the Act. The power of the court to make a section 8 order is contained in section 10 of the Act.

A residence order is 'an order settling the arrangements to be made as to the person with whom a child is to live', for example:

It is ordered that the child shall live with the applicant.

The residence order is intended to reflect a more flexible and less emotive approach and to underscore the idea that residence and parental responsibility are discrete concepts. The motive behind the new notion is to make both parents feel that they have a continuing part to play in the future life of their child. It exemplifies the philosophy which lies behind the Act that children should not be perceived as the property of either parent.

In a suitable case a residence order can be made in favour of more than one person. Such a case might be where a child is in boarding school and spends part of his holidays with one parent and part with the other. Most residence orders, however, will be made in favour of one party.

If a residence order is made in favour of one parent, the other parent does not lose parental responsibility. Of course, in most cases the decisions concerning the day-to-day management or upbringing of the child will be made by the parent in whose favour the residence order has been made.

Effect of a residence order

Where a residence order is in force, no person may:

(a) cause the child to be known by a new surname *or*

(b) remove him from the UK

without either the written consent of every person who has parental responsibility for the child or the leave of the court (section 13(1)).

Note that this provision does not prevent the removal of a child, for a period of less than one month, by the person in whose favour the residence order is made (section 13(2)).

Enforcement of a residence order

Where a residence order is in force in favour of any person, and any other person (*including one in whose favour the order is also in force*) is in breach of the arrangements settled by that order, the first-mentioned person may, *as soon as a copy of the residence order has been served on the other person*, enforce the order under section 63(3) of the Magistrates' Courts Act 1980 as if it were an order requiring the other person to produce the child to him (section 14).

Contact order

A contact order is an order 'requiring the person with whom a child lives, or is to live, to allow the child to visit or stay with the person named in the order, or for that person and the child otherwise to have contact with each other'.

Is it not the old access order in different language?

No, for several reasons. First, there is a shift to the child from the adult, in keeping with the philosophy behind the Act which is 'child-centred'. Secondly, the contact implicit in the new order is wider in its scope in that it contemplates contact between the child and any other person – not just a parent – and can include telephoning and contact by letter, for example:

It is further ordered that the child shall stay with the respondent every weekend from 6 p.m. on Fridays to 5 p.m. on Sundays commencing the 18th October 1991, visit the respondent every other Wednesday from 3.30 p.m. to 6 p.m. commencing on the 23rd October 1991 and be permitted to telephone him each Monday between 5 p.m. and 6 p.m.

A section 8 contact order is a positive order and cannot be used to prevent contact – to achieve that a prohibited steps order (see below) would have to be made.

Contact orders under section 8 must be distinguished from orders made under section 34 for contact with a child in care. Under section 34 the local authority has a statutory duty to allow the parents of a child in their care, and certain other persons close to the child, to have reasonable contact with the child. If there are problems about contact with a child in care the solution is *not* to make an application for a section 8 contact order. In fact section 9(1) specifically prevents a court from making any section 8 order (other than a residence order) with respect to a child who is the subject of a care order.

So, if a client complains about contact (he will say access) with his child, the first matter to establish is whether or not the child is the subject of a care order under section 31(1) of the Act. If the child is in care under section 31, forget about an application under section 10 for a section 8 contact order and consider section 34. (For applications for contact in respect of a child who is in care see chapter 12.)

Prohibited steps order

A 'prohibited steps order' ('PSO') means 'an order that no step which could be taken by a parent in meeting his parental responsibility for a child, and which is of a kind specified in the order, shall be taken by any person without the consent of the court'.

Both this order and the specific issue order below are modelled on the wardship jurisdiction. Two aspects of the new order are worth noting at this stage: first, a PSO may be made against anyone – a stranger who is thought to be a bad influence, for example – and, secondly, the order can only be used to prohibit a step which could be taken by a parent in meeting his parental responsibility. So, for example, the court could not make a PSO against a newspaper to restrict publicity about a child.

Specific issue order

A specific issue order is an order 'giving directions for the purpose of determining a specific question which has arisen, or which may arise, in connection with any aspect of parental responsibility for a child.' For example:

And it is further ordered that the child shall be educated at the St Heloise Convent, Abelard Grove, London N1.

Section 9(5) provides that the court should not make either a specific issue order or a PSO if the same result could be achieved by making a residence order or a contact order. If the court decides, therefore, that a child should live with his mother rather than his father, that arrangement should be achieved by making a residence order in favour of mother rather than making an order prohibiting the child from living with his father.

8.2 PRELIMINARY ENQUIRIES

Is a separate application in the family proceedings court necessary?

If there are family proceedings (see chapter 1) in any other court, you should issue your application in those proceedings rather than commence separate proceedings. You should ask your client, therefore, if he is aware of any other proceedings involving the child.

Age of the child

If the child has reached 16 years the court cannot make any section 8 order (other than one varying or discharging an existing order) unless the circumstances are exceptional (section 9(7)).

Local authority as applicant

A local authority cannot apply for a residence order, or a contact order and no court shall make such an order in favour of a local authority (section 9(2)).

Nor shall a court make any section 8 order, other than a residence order, with respect to a child who is in the care of a local authority (section 9(1)).

Section 9(1) does not apply, however, where the child is being 'accommodated' by a local authority, so an authority may in an appropriate case obtain a PSO or specific issue order in respect of a child who is being accommodated by them.

Leave to apply

The following *do not need leave* of the court to apply for either a residence order or a contact order under section 8:

(a)   any parent or guardian of the child (section 10(4)(a))

(b)   any person in whose favour a residence order is in force (section 10(4)(b))

(c)   any spouse or ex-spouse in relation to a child of the family (section 10(5)(a))

(d)   any person with whom the child has lived for at least three years out of the last five years provided the child did not cease to live with the applicant more than three months ago (section 10(5)(b) and section 10)

(e)   where there is already a residence order in force, anyone who has the consent of each person in whose favour the order was made (section 10(5)(c)(i))

(f)   where the child is in care, anyone who has the consent of the local authority concerned (section 10(5)(c)(ii))

(g)   anyone who has the consent of those who have parental responsibility for the child (section 10(5)(c)(iii))

(h)   any person who falls within a category of persons prescribed by rules of court (the rules will probably provide for grandparents to apply without leave).

The following persons can apply for a PSO or a specific issue order *without leave*:

(a)   any parent or guardian of the child (section 10(4)(a))

(b)   any person in whose favour a residence order is in force (section 10(4)(b))

(c)   persons in categories specifically prescribed by rules of court (section 10(7)).

Anyone falling outside the above must apply for leave (see chapter 5).

Child as client

The child may apply for any section 8 order, but only with leave. Leave may only be granted if the court is satisfied that the child is of 'sufficient understanding to make the proposed application' (section 10(8)).

Chapter 9

Making the Section 8 Application

9.1 INTRODUCTION

As with all applications made in the family proceedings court the procedure is governed by the Family Proceedings Courts (Children Act 1989) Rules 1991 ('the Rules'). You should follow the steps set out in chapter 2.

9.2 FILLING IN THE FORM

The appropriate form for an application for a residence order, a contact order, a PSO and a specific issue order is Form CHA 10 and you will find this on pages 43 to 50 inclusive of the Rules.

The form contains nine sections including the declaration and a notice of hearing. It is mostly self-explanatory and is designed so that as much information about the application as possible is conveyed in the form itself to the court and to all parties concerned (for an example of a completed form see the end of this chapter).

(As a safeguard, to ensure that an application is not made in the family proceedings court when one of the parties has commenced proceedings for divorce, Form CHA 10 declares: 'Do not use this form if you are the petitioner or respondent to divorce proceedings. Use Form CHA 10(D)'. Form CHA 10(D) is to be found in the appendix to the Family Proceedings Rules 1991 which govern proceedings in the county court and High Court.)

You need one form for each respondent (see below) *and you need to fill in a separate form for each child in respect of whom you are seeking an order.*

You are also required to fill in parts of Form CHA 10A (respondent's answer). The format of CHA 10A suggests that it is the applicant who must serve that form on each respondent.

9.3 RESPONDENTS

The respondents are:

(a) every person whom you believe to have parental responsibility for the child (for parental responsibility see chapter 7)

(b) if the child is the subject of a care order, every person whom you believe had parental responsibility immediately prior to the making of the care order

(c) if the child is the subject of a care order and the section 8 order sought is a residence order, the child himself.

9.4 FILING THE APPLICATION

See chapter 2.

9.5 SERVICE

You must serve all the documents at least *21 days* before the hearing or directions appointment (see column (ii) of Schedule 2 to the Rules on page 214 of the Rules). Remember to file a statement of service – see chapter 2.

9.6 GIVING NOTICE

Under the Rules you must give *written notice* of the application and of the date, time and place of the hearing or directions appointment to:

(a) where applicable, the local authority providing accommodation for the child

(b)   where applicable, any person caring for the child at the time when the application is commenced

(c)   in the case of proceedings brought in respect of a child who is alleged to be staying in a certificated refuge, the person who is providing the refuge

(d)   every person whom you believe to be named in a court order with respect to the child which has not ceased to exist, unless you believe that the court order is not relevant to the application

(e)   every person whom you believe to be a party to pending proceedings in respect of the child unless you believe that the pending proceedings are not relevant to the application

(f)   every person whom you believe to be a person with whom the child has lived for at least three years prior to the making of the application.

There appears to be no particular form for giving the written notice.

9.7   RESPONDENT'S ANSWER

Rule 9 provides that within 14 days of service of an application for a section 8 order the respondent 'shall' (so it is mandatory) serve on the parties an answer to the application in the appropriate form. You will find the appropriate form (CHA 10A) on pages 51 and 52 of the Rules. For an example of a completed CHA 10A see the end of this chapter. Do not forget that it is the applicant's job to send CHA 10A to each respondent.

O
Y **CHA 10**
E **Application for a Contact Order, Prohibited Steps Order,**
Z **Residence Order or Specific Issue Order**

Section 10 The Children Act 1989

Date received by Court

♦ Please use black ink. The notes on page 7 tell you what to do when you have completed the form.

♦ Please answer every part. If a part does not apply or you do not know what to say, please say so. If there is not enough room continue on another sheet (put the child's name and the number of the part on the sheet).

♦ If there is more than one child you must fill in a separate form for each child.

♦ If you have any concerns about giving your address or that of the child or any other address requested in this form, you may give an alternative address where papers can be served. However, you must notify the Court of the actual address on a separate form available from the Court.

> Please speak to the court official immediately if you wish an application for a specific issue or prohibited steps order to be heard without giving Notice of the application to any other party.

━━━━ THE ━━━ CHILDREN ━━━ ACT ━━━

I apply to The *BARCHESTER*   [High] [County] [Magistrates'] Court

Case No.

for a   * contact order   * prohibited steps order
             * residence order   * specific issue order   (*delete which does not apply)

♦ Do not use this form if you are the petitioner or respondent to divorce proceedings. Use form CHA 10 (D).

♦ If you are making this application within any other family proceedings, please state case number of those related proceedings.

━━━━ THE ━━━ CHILDREN ━━━ ACT ━━━

1 About the child

(a) The full name of the child is   *JANE TOWNSEND*
    Put the surname last.

(b) The child is a   ☐ boy   ☑ girl

(c) The child was born on the   *27*day *AUGUST*month *1981*year   Age now *10 years*

(d) The child usually lives at   *10, ST. JOHN'S VILLAS*
    See note on addresses at top   *LITTLE BARCHESTER*
    of this page   *WESSEX*

(e) The child lives with   ☑ the child's mother   ☐ the child's father   *MARIA TOWNSEND*
    If the child is not with a parent
    give the name of the person
    who is responsible for the child.

(f) The child is also cared for by   *DEREK ROBINSON*
    Put the surname last.

(g) The carer is the child's   *MOTHER (MR ROBINSON-STEPFATHER)*
    Put the relationship of the
    carer to the child.

(h) The child is at present   ☐ staying in a refuge
                                         (Please give the address to the Court separately)
                                         ☑ not staying in a refuge

(i) If the child is temporarily   *N/A*
    living away from the usual
    address please say where
    he/she is living at present.
    See note on addresses at top
    of this page

━━━ THE ━━━ CHILDREN ━━━ ACT ━━━

1

2 About myself (the person applying)

(a) I am
- [ ] the child
- [✓] the child's ~~mother or~~ father
- [ ] a guardian of the child
- [ ] a person with parental responsibility *(see part 4 of form)*
- [ ] none of the above. I am _____

(b) Leave to make this application
(complete only if leave is required)
- [ ] is being sought
- [ ] has been given. The Court which gave leave was

N/A   Case No.

Leave was given on   day   month   year

(c) My title is
- [✓] Mr
- [ ] Mrs
- [ ] Miss
- [ ] Ms
- [ ] Other *(say here)*

(d) My full name is
Put the surname last.

KEVIN REYNOLDS

(e) My address is
See note on addresses at top of page 1.

12 MANOR ROAD GREATER BARCHESTER WESSEX

(f) My telephone number is

0931 445 756

(g) My Solicitor for these proceedings is

Name *I am acting in person*
Address

Tel. *See above*   Fax *N/A*   Ref.

═══ THE ▬▬ CHILDREN ▬▬ ACT ═══

3 About the child's family

(a) The name of the child's mother is
Put the surname last.

MARIA TOWNSEND

(b) The mother usually lives at
See note on addresses at top of page 1.

10, ST. JOHN'S VILLAS LITTLE BARCHESTER WESSEX

(c) The full name of the child's father is
Put the surname last.

KEVIN REYNOLDS

(d) The father usually lives at
See note on addresses at top of page 1.

See above

2

3 About the child's family (continued)

(e) The child's mother and father   ☐ are living together   ☑ are living apart

(f) The father is   ☐ married to the child's mother   ☑ married to someone else

     ☐ single   ☐ divorced

(g) The mother is   ☐ married to the child's father   ☑ married to someone else

     ☐ single   ☐ divorced

(h) The child has   ☐ no brothers and sisters under 18

     ☑ brothers and sisters under 18. They are

See note on addresses at the top of page 1.

Put the names, addresses and ages of all full brothers and sisters.

If the child has halfbrothers or halfsisters, stepbrothers or stepsisters say who they are in (i) below.

If there are other children who are treated as children of the family say who they are in (i) below.

Do not include adoption orders.

The name(s) of the brother(s) and sister(s)	Age (years)	The address(es) of the brother(s) and sister(s)
TOBY CLARK	14	10, ST. JOHN'S VILLAS LITTLE BARCHESTER WESSEX

☑ No order has been made for any brother or sister

☐ No order for a brother or sister has been applied for

☐ An order has been made for a brother or sister

☐ An order for a brother or sister has been applied for

The name(s) of the child(ren)	The type of order	The court which made the order and when or which will hear the application and the case number if known	✓ has been applied for	if the order is in force
N/A	N/A	N/A		

(i) There are other children   ☐ under 18 who do not live with the family

     ☐ under 18 who live with the family

They are: *See note on addresses at top of page 1.*

The name of the child	The age of the child	Please give reasons why the child lives/ does not live with the family	Address of child not living with the family
N/A	N/A	N/A	N/A

3 About the child's family (continued)

☐ An order has been made for a child who lives with the family *or*

Do not include adoption orders. ☐ An order for a child who lives with the family has been applied for

The name(s) of the child(ren)	The type of order	The court which made the order and when or which will hear the application and the case number if known	✓ has been applied for	if the order is in force
N/A	*N/A*	*N/A*		

━━━━ THE ▬▬ CHILDREN ▬▬ ACT ━━━━

4 Parental responsibility

Some people have "parental responsibility" for a child.
The law says what "parental responsibility" is
and which people have it. These people include:

A   the mother

B   the father
if he was married to the child's mother
when the child was born

C   the father
*if he was **not** married to the child's mother*
when the child was born
but he now has a residence order

or   he now has a court order
which gives him parental responsibility

or   he now has a formal "parental responsibility
agreement" with the mother

or   he has since married the mother

D   a guardian of the child

E   someone who holds a custody or residence order

F   a local authority which has a care order

G   someone who holds an emergency protection order

H   any man or woman who has adopted the child

I believe the people who have parental
responsibility for this child are.

See note on addresses at the top of page 1.

Name	Address
MARIA TOWNSEND	10, ST. JOHN'S VILLAS LITTLE BARCHESTER WESSEX

━━━━ THE ▬▬ CHILDREN ▬▬ ACT ━━━━

4

5 | About court proceedings and the parents

Please give details of any
relevant proceedings involving
the parents and/or those with
parental responsibility.
Include the name of the court
and the case number.

☑ Proceedings are not pending or in progress

☐ Proceedings are pending or in progress

━━━ THE ━━━ CHILDREN ━━━ ACT ━━━

6 | About other applications and orders which affect the child

(a) An Emergency Protection Order

☑ is not in force

☐ is in force. The court which made the order was

> *N/A*

Case No. | *N/A*

The Order ends on | *N/A*

(b) Other applications have

☑ not been made

☐ been made or will be made

When an application was made or will be made	What the application was for or will be for	The court which heard the application or which will hear the application and the case number if known	The result
N/A	*N/A*	*N/A*	*N/A*

6 About other applications and orders which affect the child (continued)

(c) Other orders   ☑ have not been made

☐ have been made. (Do not include adoption orders)

The orders are

The type of order	When the order was made	The court which made the order and the case number if known	✓ if the order has expired say when	is in force
N/A	*N/A*	*N/A*		

━━━ THE ━━━ CHILDREN ━━━ ACT ━━━

7 About this application

(a) I wish the Court to order that

Give details of the order and of any other directions you would like the court to make.

My daughter Jane should be allowed to stay with me every other weekend from Saturday morning until Sunday evening, and to visit me every Wednesday from 3·45 pm until 8·00 pm. I would also like to be able to speak to her over the telephone.

(b) I am making this application because

(i) You should only put your reasons for applying in this section.

(ii) You should put your plans for the future care of the child in Part 7 (c) where relevant.

Maria Townsend and I lived together for several years. Following our separation I used to see Jane regularly. Two months ago, Maria married Derek Robinson. Since then I have not been allowed to see my daughter. I believe that it is in Jane's best interest to see me on a regular basis.

6

7 | About this application (continued)

(c)   My plans for the child are
Where relevant give your plans for the future care of the child.
Please say where the child should live and whom the child should see or should not see.

N/A

━━━━━━━━━ THE ━━ CHILDREN ━━ ACT ━━━━━━━━━

8 | The respondents

The respondent(s) will be

● all those with parental responsibility [see part 4].

● If the child is the subject of a care order, all those who had parental responsibility for the child immediately before the care order was made.

● other persons allowed by the Rules of Court.

(i) You need not give details of those respondents whose names and addresses have been given in part 4.

(ii) Please put the address where the respondent usually lives or can be served with papers. See note on addresses at the top of page 1.

(iii) You will have to serve a copy of this application on each of the respondents.

The name of the respondent	The respondent's address

━━━━━━━━━ THE ━━ CHILDREN ━━ ACT ━━━━━━━━━

9 | Declaration

I declare that the information I have given is correct and complete to the best of my knowledge.

Signed   *K. Reynolds*   Date   *7th October 1991*

━━━━━━━━━ THE ━━ CHILDREN ━━ ACT ━━━━━━━━━

What you (the person applying) must do next

▶ There is a Notice of Hearing on page 8. Fill in the boxes on the Notice.

▶ Take or send this form to the court with enough copies for each respondent to be served. The top copy will be kept by the court and the other copies given or sent back to you for service.

▶ You **must** then serve the copies of the Application and the Notice of Hearing according to the Rules. You may also be required under the Rules to give notice of the proceedings to other people.

━━━━━━━━━ THE ━━ CHILDREN ━━ ACT ━━━━━━━━━

In the   [High] [County] [Magistrates'] Court

at

(When writing to the court please state the Case No.)   **Case No.**

Tel.   Fax

THE ▬ CHILDREN ▬ ACT

Notice of a [Hearing] [Directions Appointment]

You are named as a Respondent in these proceedings

Name of the child   *JANE TOWNSEND*
Put the surname last.

☐ a boy   ☑ a girl

born on the   *27 August 1981*

You must read this Notice now

THE ▬ CHILDREN ▬ ACT

About the [Hearing] [Directions Appointment]   name of applicant

KEVIN REYNOLDS

has made an application to the Court.

The Court has been asked to make   ☑ a contact order   ☐ a residence order

☐ a prohibited steps order   ☐ a specific issue order

THE ▬ CHILDREN ▬ ACT

To be completed by the Court

The Court will hear this at

on

at   o'clock

the time allowed is

THE ▬ CHILDREN ▬ ACT

WHAT YOU MUST DO

▶ There is a copy of the application with this Notice. Read the application now. You do not have to fill in any part.

▶ You must complete the form of Answer enclosed and follow the instructions on the first page of the Answer regarding service.

▶ You should obtain legal advice from a solicitor or, alternatively, from an advice agency. The Law Society administers a national panel of solicitors to represent children and other parties involved in proceedings relating to children. Addresses of solicitors (including panel members) and advice agencies can be obtained from the Yellow Pages and the Solicitors Regional Directory which can be found at Citizens Advice Bureaux, Law Centres and any local library. A solicitor or advice agency will also be able to advise you as to whether you will be eligible for legal aid.

date

8

OYEZ   The Solicitors' Law Stationery Society Ltd., Oyez House, 7 Spa Road, London SE16 3QQ   8 91 F20635

CHA 10   5037577

In the *BARCHESTER*   [High] [County] [Magistrates'] Court

at *14 HIGH STREET, BARCHESTER, WESSEX*

(When writing to the court please state the Case No.)   **Case No.**

Tel. *BARCHESTER 427925* Fax *0931 427924*

━━━━ THE ━━━ CHILDREN ━━━ ACT ━━━━

To the applicant: before you send this form you must insert the name and address of the Respondent and the name of the child in the relevant boxes below.

Respondent's name and address

> *MARIA TOWNSEND*
> *10, ST JOHN'S VILLAS,*
> *LITTLE BARCHESTER,*
> *WESSEX*

━━━━ THE ━━━ CHILDREN ━━━ ACT ━━━━

Respondent's Answer

The full name of the child is
Put the surname last.
| *JANE TOWNSEND* |

You will get with this form a copy of

◗ a Notice of Hearing
   or Directions Appointment

◗ an application that has been made to the court

Please

◗ read the Notice first

◗ then read the application

◗ answer the questions on this form

You must return only this Answer to the court and serve a copy on the applicant and each respondent (see parts 4 and 8 of the application form) within 14 days from the date of service.

━━━━ THE ━━━ CHILDREN ━━━ ACT ━━━━

To the court: insert name and address of court

Respondent's Answer   Case No.

Full name of child is	JANE TOWNSEND

Put the surname last.

1 | **About the application**

Please   ● read parts 1-8 of the application form before you answer the questions
● continue on another sheet if there is not enough room. Please put the case number, the name of the child and the number of the question on the sheet.

My full name is | MARIA TOWNSEND
Put the surname last.

My full address for service is | 10 ST. JOHN'S VILLAS, LITTLE BARCHESTER

Do you have legal representation?   No ☐   Yes ☑

Please say who your solicitor is

Name WRITTLE & CO

Address BANK CHAMBERS, LONDON ROAD, BARCHESTER

Tel No 0931 776   Fax 0931 770   Ref PNM

Do you accept that you should be a respondent in this application?   Yes ☑   No ☐

Please give reason then sign below

If you answer no, you need not answer a-d below.

2 | a. Is everything in the application true to the best of your knowledge?   Yes ☐   No ☑

Please explain The applicant hardly saw our daughter at all after we separated.

b. Is there anything else the court should know about this application?   No ☐   Yes ☑

Please give details Because of the applicant's lack of interest in her, Jane is now very reluctant indeed to see her father. I do not think it is in her interests to resume contact.

c. Do you agree with the applicant's plans for the child's future?   Yes ☐   No ☐

Please explain   N/A

d. Do you intend to make an application?   No ☐   Yes ☑

Please give details For maintenance of Jane

3 | I declare that the information I have given is true and correct to the best of my knowledge

Signed | Maria Townsend   Dated | 28th Oct. 1991

2

Chapter 10

Applications for Financial Provision for Children

10.1 INTRODUCTION

Schedule 1 to the Act gives the court extensive powers to make orders for financial relief with respect to children. In effect, the Schedule re-enacts (with appropriate amendments) provisions of the Guardianship of Minors Acts 1971 and 1973, the Children Act 1975 and sections 15 and 16 of the Family Law Reform Act 1987. Proceedings under Schedule 1 are classed as 'family proceedings'.

10.2 PRELIMINARIES

Who can apply?

  (a) a parent

  (b) a guardian of the child

  (c) any person in whose favour a residence order is in force with respect to a child (Schedule 1, paragraph 1(1))

  (d) a child who has attained the age of 16, if the application is for the variation or revival of a periodical payments order made to or for the benefit of the child (Schedule 1, paragraph 6(4)).

Note that the court may exercise its powers under Schedule 1, even though no application has been made for a financial provision order, when making, varying or discharging a residence order (Schedule 1, paragraph 1(6)).

What orders can be made?

The magistrates' court may order *either or both parents* to pay periodical payments and/or a lump sum to the applicant for the benefit of the child or to the child himself (Schedule 1, paragraph 1). If the applicant wants secured periodical payments, a property settlement order or a property transfer order, you will need to apply to the county court or the High Court. A lump sum in the magistrates' court may not exceed £1,000 but more than one lump sum order can be made (Schedule 1, paragraph 5(2) and (4)).

The magistrates' court may also alter a 'maintenance agreement', defined as any agreement in writing made with respect to a child which is or was made between the father and mother of the child and contains financial arrangements for the child, but *only* by inserting provision for periodical payments or varying existing provision for periodical payments *and* the application cannot be entertained unless both parties are resident in England and Wales (Schedule 1, paragraph 10).

An interim order may be made.

Duration of orders

The term specified in any order for periodical payments:

(a)   shall not in the first instance extend beyond the child's *17th birthday* unless the court thinks it right to specify a later date, and

(b)   shall not extend beyond the child's *18th birthday* (Schedule 1, paragraph 3(1)).

Child 18 or over

The court may order periodical payments to extend beyond a child's 18th birthday if it appears to the court that:

(a)   the child is or will be in further education or undergoing trade or professional training (whether or not he is in gainful employment), or

(b)   there are special circumstances which justify the making of an order (Schedule 1, paragraph 3(2)).

A child who has attained the age of 18 may make his own application for periodical payments and/or a lump sum (Schedule 1, paragraph 2) *unless*:

(a)   his parents are, at the time of the application, living in the same household

(b)   immediately before the child attained the age of 16, there was a periodical payments order in force in respect of him (Schedule 1, paragraph 2).

Criteria

The child's welfare is *not* the paramount consideration and *the checklist does not apply*.

The court must have regard to all the circumstances of the case and, in particular:

(a)   the income, earning capacity, property and other financial resources which each person mentioned in paragraph 4(4) of Schedule 1 (i.e., the parent(s), the applicant, or any other person in whose favour the court proposes to make the order) has or is likely to have in the foreseeable future

(b)   the financial needs, obligations and responsibilities which each person mentioned in paragraph 4(4) has or is likely to have in the foreseeable future

(c)   the financial needs of the child

(d)   the income, earning capacity (if any), property and other financial resources of the child

(e)   any physical or mental disability of the child

(f)   the manner in which the child was being, or was expected to be, educated or trained.

Who is a 'parent'?

'Parent' includes any party to a marriage in relation to whom the child concerned is a 'child of the family'. This does *not* apply to paragraph 2 (applications by children who have attained the age of 18) or paragraph 15 (local authority's contribution to a child's maintenance).

Respondent not mother or father of child

The court must also consider whether that person assumed responsibility for the maintenance of the child and, if so, to what extent, the basis upon which and for how long he did so, whether he did so knowing the child was not his child and the liability of any other party to maintain the child (Schedule 1, paragraph 4(2)).

10.3   MAKING THE APPLICATION

Fill in Form CHA13 which is on pages 65 to 71 of the Rules. *A separate* form is required for *each child*. A *statement of means form* (Form CHA 14 at pages 74 to 76 of the Rules) must also be completed by the applicant. Take sufficient copies of the form and the statement of means for each respondent to be served. An example of a completed CHA13 (together with CHA14) appears at the end of this chapter.

10.4   RESPONDENTS

The respondents are:

(a)   every person whom the applicant believes to have parental responsibility for the child

(b)   where the child is the subject of a care order, every person whom the applicant believes to have had parental responsibility immediately prior to the making of the care order

(c)   if applying to vary or discharge an order, the parties to the proceedings leading to the order to be varied or discharged

(d)   those persons whom the applicant believes to be interested in or affected by the proceedings.

10.5   SERVICE

Service as usual (see chapter 2) *21 days before the hearing*.

10.6   WRITTEN NOTICE

Give written notice of the proceedings and the time and place of hearing to (where applicable):

(a)   the local authority providing accommodation for the child

(b)   persons who are caring for the child at the time the proceedings are commenced

(c)   if the child is in a certificated refuge, the party providing the refuge.

10.7   ACTION TO BE TAKEN BY THE RESPONDENT

Within 14 days of service of the application, serve an *answer* in Form CHA 13A (pages 72 to 73 of the Rules) together with, if you are being asked to make any payment for the child, a *statement of means* in Form CHA 14 (pages 74 to 76).

10.8   VARIATION OR DISCHARGE

When hearing an application for variation or discharge of periodical payments, the court must have regard to all the circumstances of the case, including any change in the matters to which it had regard when making the order. The court may *suspend temporarily* a periodical payments order or *revive* any order so suspended (paragraph 6(2) of Schedule 1). The application is in Form CHA 15 (pages 77 to 79 of the Rules).

10.9   ENFORCEMENT

An order for payment of money under the Act is enforceable as a magistrates' maintenance order within the meaning of section 150(1) of the Magistrates' Courts Act 1980.

Any person required by a magistrates' court order to pay money under the Act must give notice of his change of address to such person (if any) as may be specified in the order. A failure without reasonable cause to give such notice constitutes a summary offence.

10.10 FINANCIAL RELIEF UNDER OTHER ENACTMENTS

If a residence order is made at a time when there is already in existence an order made otherwise than under the Act requiring a person to contribute to a child's maintenance, the court can, on the application of the contributor or the person with whom the child is to reside, revoke or vary the order.

10.11 EXISTING POWERS

The courts may still make orders for the benefit of children of a marriage under the Matrimonial Causes Act 1973 and the Domestic Proceedings and Magistrates' Courts Act 1978.

CHA 13

O
Y
E
Z

Application for Financial Provision for Children

Schedule 1 The Children Act 1989

Date received by Court

♦ Please use black ink. The notes on page 6 tell you what to do when you have completed the form.

♦ If there is more than one child you must fill in a separate form for each child.

♦ Please answer every part. If a part does not apply or you do not know what to say please say so. If there is not enough room continue on another sheet (put the child's name and the number of the part on the sheet).

♦ If you have any concerns about giving your address or that of the child or any other address requested in this form, you may give an alternative address where papers can be served. However, you must notify the Court of the actual address on a separate form available from the Court.

━━━━━ THE ━━━━━ CHILDREN ━━━━━ ACT ━━━━━

I apply to The   *BARCHESTER*   [High] [County] [Magistrates'] Court

                                                  Case No.

for an order for

- [✓] periodical payments
- [ ] secured periodical payments*
- [ ] lump sum
- [ ] settlement of property*
- [ ] transfer of property*

*these orders can only be made in the High Court or a county court

━━━━━ THE ━━━━━ CHILDREN ━━━━━ ACT ━━━━━

1 About the child

(a) The name of the child is
Put the surname last.

JANE TOWNSEND

(b) The child is a   [ ] boy [✓] girl

(c) The child was born on the   *27* day *August* month *1981* year   Age now *10 years*

(d) The child usually lives at
See note on addresses at top of this form.

10, ST. JOHN'S VILLAS, LITTLE BARCHESTER, WESSEX

(e) The child lives with
If the child does not live with a parent please give the name of the person who is responsible for the child.

[✓] the child's mother   [ ] the child's father

(f) The child is also cared for by
Put the surname last.

DEREK ROBINSON

(g) The child is at present

[ ] staying in a refuge (Please give the address to the Court separately)

[✓] not staying in a refuge

(h) The child usually lives at
If the child is temporarily living away from usual address please say where he/she is living at present.

See note on addresses at top of this form.

See above

━━━━━ THE ━━━━━ CHILDREN ━━━━━ ACT ━━━━━

1

2 About myself (the person applying)

(a) I am

- [ ] the child (if 18 or over)
- [x] the child's mother ~~or father~~
- [ ] a guardian of the child
- [ ] a person with a residence order
- [ ] none of the above. I am _____

(b) Leave to make this application
Only complete if leave is required.

- [ ] is being sought
- [ ] has been given. The Court which gave leave was

_____

Leave was given on | day | month | year |

(c) My title is

- [ ] Mr [ ] Mrs [ ] Miss [x] Ms [ ] Other *(say here)* _____

(d) My full name is
Put the surname last.

MARIA TOWNSEND

(e) My full address is
See note on addresses at top of page 1.

10, ST JOHN'S VILLAS,
LITTLE BARCHESTER,
WESSEX

(f) My telephone number is

BARCHESTER 59297

(g) My Solicitor is

Name WRITTLE & CO
Address BANK CHAMBERS
LONDON ROAD
BARCHESTER

Tel. 0931 776 Fax 0931 770 Ref. PNM

THE ■ CHILDREN ■ ACT

3 About the child's family

(a) The name of the child's mother is
Put the surname last.

MARIA TOWNSEND

(b) The mother usually lives at
See note on addresses at top of page 1.

10, ST. JOHN'S VILLAS,
LITTLE BARCHESTER,
WESSEX

(c) The name of the child's father is
Put the surname last.

KEVIN REYNOLDS

(d) The father usually lives at
See note on addresses at top of page 1

12, MANOR ROAD
GREATER BARCHESTER
WESSEX

2

3 About the child's family (continued)

(e) The child's mother and father ☐ are living together ☑ are living apart

(f) The father is ☐ married to the child's mother ☐ married to someone else

☑ single ☐ divorced

(g) The mother is ☐ married to the child's father ☑ married to someone else

☐ single ☐ divorced

━━━━━ THE ━━━━ CHILDREN ━━━━ ACT ━━━━

4 Parental responsibility

Some people have "parental responsibility" for a child.
The law says what "parental responsibility" is
and which people have it. These people include:

A the mother

B the father
    if he was married to the child's mother
    when the child was born

C the father
    if he was **not** married to the child's mother
    when the child was born
        but he now has a residence order
        or he now has a court order
            which gives him parental responsibility
        or he now has a formal "parental responsibility
            agreement" with the mother
        or he has since married the mother

D a guardian of the child

E someone who holds a custody or residence order

F a local authority which has a care order

G someone who holds an emergency protection order

H any man or woman who has adopted the child

Name	Address
Maria Townsend	*10, ST. JOHN'S VILLAS, LITTLE BARCHESTER WESSEX*

The people who are believed
to have parental
responsibility for this
child are

*See note on addresses at the
top of page 1.*

━━━━━ THE ━━━━ CHILDREN ━━━━ ACT ━━━━

5 About court proceedings and the parents

Please give details of any relevant court proceedings between the parents and/or those who have parental responsibility.

Include the name of the Court and the case number of the proceedings if known.

☐ Proceedings are not pending or in progress.
☑ Proceedings are pending or in progress.
Please give details below.

> Kevin Reynolds is applying for a contact order in respect of Jane, in the Barchester Magistrates' Court

THE ■ CHILDREN ■ ACT ■

6 About this application

(a) I wish the Court to order that

Give details of the financial provision you wish the Court to make, including the amounts requested.

> Kevin Reynolds should make periodical payments to Jane in the sum of £40 per week

(b) The financial needs of the child are

Apart from Jane's everyday needs she has weekly piano lessons at a cost of £7.50 per lesson; she also goes horse-riding every Saturday at a cost of £4.00

(c) The income, earnings capacity (if any), property and other financial resources of the child are

Jane is not in receipt of any income.

(d) State if the child has any physical or mental disability. If yes, please give details

☑ no
☐ yes

6 About this application (continued)

(e) The manner in which the child is being, or is expected to be, educated or trained.

> Jane will continue to attend her present school for one more year and then will go to Barchester Grammar School until she is 18 years old .

(f) You should now complete the statement of means form (CHA 14).

THE CHILDREN ACT

7 The respondents

The respondent(s) will be all those who
- have parental responsibility
- are interested in or affected by the proceedings
- are allowed by Rules of Court

(i) Only give the names and addresses of those people whose details are not given in part 4 of this form.

(ii) Please put the address where the respondent usually lives or where papers can be served. See note on addresses at the top of page 1.

(iii) You will have to serve a copy of this application on each of the respondents.

The name of the respondent	The respondent's address
Derek Robinson	10, St. John's Villas, Little Barchester, Wessex .

THE CHILDREN ACT

8 Declaration

I declare that the information I have given is correct and complete to the best of my knowledge.

Signed *Maria Townsend*

Date *28th October 1991*

THE CHILDREN ACT

What you (the person applying) must do next

- There is a Notice of Hearing on page 7. Fill in the boxes on the Notice.

- Take or send this form and statement of means to the Court with enough copies for each respondent to be served. The top copy will be kept by the Court and the other copies given or sent back to you for service.

- You **must** then serve the copies of the Application, the Notice of Hearing, the statement of means and the Respondent's Answer according to the Rules. You may also be required under the Rules to give notice of the proceedings to other people.

In the *BARCHESTER*   [High] [County] [Magistrates'] Court

at *14, HIGH STREET, BARCHESTER, WESSEX*

(When writing to the Court please state the Case No.)   **Case No.**

Tel. *BARCHESTER 427 925*   Fax *0931 427 924*

▬▬▬ THE ▬▬▬ CHILDREN ▬▬▬ ACT ▬▬▬

Notice of a [Hearing] [Directions Appointment]

You are named as a Respondent in these proceedings

about the child

> *JANE TOWNSEND*
>
> ☐ a boy   ☑ a girl

born on the

> *27 August 1981*

You must read this Notice now

▬▬▬ THE ▬▬▬ CHILDREN ▬▬▬ ACT ▬▬▬

About the [Hearing] [Directions Appointment]   *name of applicant*

> *MARIA TOWNSEND*

has made an application to the Court.

The Court has been asked to make an order for financial provision for the child

▬▬▬ THE ▬▬▬ CHILDREN ▬▬▬ ACT ▬▬▬

To be completed by the Court

The Court will hear this at

on

at   o'clock

the time allowed is

▬▬▬ THE ▬▬▬ CHILDREN ▬▬▬ ACT ▬▬▬

WHAT YOU MUST DO

♦ There is a copy of the application and statement of means with this Notice. Read the application **now**. You do not have to fill in any part. You must complete the form of Answer enclosed and follow the instructions on the first page of the Answer regarding service.

♦ You should obtain legal advice from a solicitor or, alternatively, from an advice agency. The Law Society administers a national panel of solicitors to represent children and other parties involved in proceedings relating to children. Addresses of solicitors (including panel members) and advice agencies can be obtained from the Yellow Pages and the Solicitors Regional Directory which can be found at Citizens Advice Bureaux, Law Centres and any local library. A solicitor or advice agency will also be able to advise you as to whether you will be eligible for legal aid.

date

▬▬▬ THE ▬▬▬ CHILDREN ▬▬▬ ACT ▬▬▬

O CHA 14
Y
E Statement of Means
Z
Schedule 1   The Children Act 1989

Date received by court

♦ Please use black ink.

♦ Please complete all parts of the form which apply to you.

♦ Continue on a separate sheet if necessary, stating the name of the child, case number and number of the part on each sheet.

In the *BARCHESTER*

[High] [County] [Magistrates'] Court

Case No:

━━━━━ THE ━━━ CHILDREN ━━━ ACT ━━━

1 Personal details

Surname	*TOWNSEND*
Forename(s)	*MARIA*

☐ Mr.   ☐ Mrs.   ☐ Miss   ☑ Ms.   ☐ Other
☑ Married   ☐ Single   ☐ Other *(specify)*

Age *39*

Address *10, ST. JOHN'S VILLAS LITTLE BARCHESTER WESSEX*

Postcode

I am ☑ the applicant in these proceedings

☐ the respondent in these proceedings

2 Dependants *(people you support financially)*

Children living with you

Name(s)	Age
TOBY CLARK	*14*
JANE TOWNSEND	*10*

Children not living with you (excluding those in respect of whom these proceedings are being brought)

Name(s)	Age
N/A	

Amount of any maintenance being paid

NONE

Other dependants
(give details —including whether you have these responsibilities on a part-time basis)

N/A

3 Employment

I am ☐ employed as a

☐ self employed as a

☑ unemployed

☐ a pensioner

My employer is
State name and address

N/A

Jobs other than main job

N/A

Self employment annual turnover   £ *N/A*

☑ I am not in arrears with my national insurance contributions, income tax and VAT

☐ I am in arrears and I owe   £

Give details of contracts and other work in hand

N/A

Give details of any sums due in respect of work done

N/A

4   **Bank accounts and savings**

(a) I have ☐1 ~~bank or~~ building society account(s)

Name of account	Average balance in a/c over last 6 months
WESSEX BUILDING SOCIETY ACCOUNT	£ 150·00

(b) I have ☐ savings account(s)

Name of account	Amount in account
N/A	

When filling in sections 6, 7 and 9, please give amounts on a weekly OR monthly basis. Do NOT put some weekly and some monthly figures.

5   **Property**

(b) I live in ☐ my own property

☐ lodgings

☐ jointly owned property

☑ council property

☐ privately rented property

☐ other. Please state

Value of (jointly) owned property   £ N/A

6   **Income**   Amounts are per week/month*
*Delete as appropriate

My usual take home pay *(including overtime, commission, bonuses etc)*	£
Income support	£
Child benefit(s)	£ 14·50
Other state benefit(s)	£
My pension(s)	£
Others living in my home give me	£ 60·00
Other income *(give details below)*	
the £60 comes from	£ 40·00
Derek and he also pays	£
the rent of £40	£
Total income	£ 114·50

2

7 Expenses *(do not include any payments made by other members of the household out of their own income)*

I have regular expenses as follows: *(do not include payments on any arrears).*

Amounts are per week/~~month~~ *Delete as appropriate.*

Mortgage *(including second mortgage)*	£
Rent	£ 40.00
Community charge	£ 4.00
Gas	£ 15.00
Electricity	£ 4.00
Water charges	£ 3.50
TV rental and licence	£ 2.50
HP repayments	£ NONE
Mail order	£ 4.50
Housekeeping, food, school meals	£ 60.00
Travelling expenses	£ NONE
Children's clothing and pocket money	£ 5.00
Maintenance payments	£
Others (but not credit debt payments or court orders)	
	£
	£
	£
Total expenses	**£ 140.50**

8 Court orders

Court	Case No.	Amount outstanding	Payment per month
NONE			

9 Money you owe on essential bills

Please state the amount of any arrears owing and the amount of any payments you make towards these arrears.

Payments are per week/month* *Delete as appropriate*

	Total amount outstanding	Amount of payments
Rent	£ NONE	
Mortgage	£ N/A	
Community charge	£ NONE	
Water rates	£ NONE	
Fuel debts: Gas	£ 120 arrears	
Electricity	£ NONE	
Other	£ NONE	
Maintenance arrears	£ NONE	
Total priority debts	**£ 120—00**	

10 Other commitments

Give details of payments on any credit cards, other loans, storecards, loans from family etc

	Total amount outstanding	Payment per month
	£	
	£	
	£ N/A	
	£	
	£	
	£	
Total	**£**	

11 Declaration

I declare that the details I have given above are true to the best of my knowledge

Signed *Maria Townsend*

Dated 28 Oct. '91

3

Chapter 11

Applications for a Care Order or a Supervision Order

11.1 INTRODUCTION

This chapter is concerned with the public law orders which are available to the court in relation to the care and supervision of children.

No child may be placed in the care of a local authority or put under the supervision of a local authority except by action under the scheme set out in the Act. In particular the use of the High Court's inherent jurisdiction to put a child into local authority care is abolished (section 100(2)(a)).

11.2 PRELIMINARIES

Who can bring proceedings?

Only a *local authority* or an authorised person. The only 'authorised person' at the moment is the NSPCC, which includes any of its officers (see section 31(9)). The police can no longer initiate such proceedings. But note that where the NSPCC proposes making an application it *must* consult the local authority in whose area the child is normally resident before making the application if it is reasonably practicable to do so (section 31(6)).

What is a care order?

A care order is an order placing the child with respect to whom the application is made in the care of a designated local authority (section 31(1)(a)).

What is a supervision order?

A supervision order is an order placing the child under the supervision of a designated local authority or of a probation officer (section 31(1)(b)).

Venue

Care and supervision proceedings are 'family proceedings' and for the first time they can be heard in the High Court and the county court as well as in the magistrates' court.

However, most care proceedings and proceedings for a supervision order will begin in the magistrates' court (article 3 of the Children (Allocation of Proceedings) Order 1991) (but see chapter 2 under 'Venue'). That requirement does not mean that the proceedings must stay in the magistrates' court. After they have been commenced careful consideration will have to be given to the question of whether the proceedings should be transferred. The criteria set out in the Order must be applied. The issue of when the proceedings should be transferred is considered in chapter 3, but it is inconceivable that a serious sexual abuse case, for example, would remain in the magistrates' court. Cooperation and candour will be necessary on the part of everyone concerned with the proceedings at an early stage if delay is to be avoided.

11.3   CRITERIA

Threshold criteria

Under section 31(2) of the Act, before making either a care order or a supervision order the court must be satisfied:

(a)   that the child concerned is suffering or is likely to suffer *significant* harm

and

(b)   that the harm (or likelihood of harm) is attributable to *either*:

(i)   the fact that the care which is being given to the child (or likely to be given to him if the order is not made) is not the sort of care you would expect a reasonable parent to give to him; *or*

(ii)   the fact that the child is *beyond parental control.*

These have been called the 'threshold criteria'. It is plain from the wording of section 31(2) that the court is entitled to consider making appropriate orders in cases where harm has not yet been suffered by the child in question, but where there is a *likelihood* of such harm.

Harm

Harm is defined in section 31(9) of the Act as 'ill-treatment or the impairment of health or development'. Where the question of whether harm suffered by a child is significant turns on the the child's health or development, his health or development shall be compared with that which could reasonably be expected of a similar child (section 31(10)).

Ill-treatment

Ill-treatment is defined (section 31(9)) as including sexual abuse and forms of ill-treatment which are not physical.

Minor ill-treatment

It is generally agreed that any ill-treatment would have to be significant, so minor ill-treatment would not be sufficient to satisfy this limb of the criteria.

Health

Section 31(9) provides that health means 'physical or mental health'.

Development

Development means 'physical, intellectual, emotional, social or behavioural development' (section 31(9)).

Third party

If a child suffers harm at the hands of someone other than a parent, intervention under section 31 is not justified (unless a parent is failing to prevent such harm).

Such a situation may justify intervention under a different part of the Act, for example, an application for an emergency protection order (section 44 – see chapter 14), or a child assessment order (section 43 – see chapter 15).

Age of child

If the child has reached the age of *17* years, neither a care order nor a supervision order can be made (section 31(3)). If the child is married the court cannot make such orders in respect of him once he has attained the age of *16* years.

The welfare principle

The welfare principle applies, as does the checklist and the presumption *against* making an order.

11.4 THE APPLICATION

As with all applications made in the family proceedings court the procedure is governed by the Family Proceedings Courts (Children Act 1989) Rules 1991 ('the Rules'). For the procedure to be followed when making an application under section 31, see generally chapter 2.

Filling in the form

Fill in Form CHA 19 which is to be found on pages 88 to 96 of the Rules. (For a completed example, see the end of this chapter.)

CHA 19 consists of nine sections. Sections 7 and 8 are of particular importance because they require the local authority to set out its reasons for seeking either the care order or the supervision order. It will be important to draft reasons carefully and fully. There is much more emphasis under the new law on providing as much information as possible before the hearing so that all parties know the case they have to answer and are not taken by surprise.

Section 8 of the form requires the local authority to state its plans for the child from the outset. This means that before care proceedings are commenced the local authority should have a clear idea of how it sees the child's future and how it intends to implement its plans. To oblige the local authority to focus on what it intends to do with the child will compel a consideration of all the options. It may conclude that care proceedings are unnecessary and that the family should be assisted in some of the other ways contemplated by the Act.

Under the Act (section 17) local authorities are under a general duty to promote the upbringing of children in need by their families so far as this is consistent with the duty to safeguard and promote the welfare of such children. The local authority should carefully explore whether voluntary co-operation with the parents and the provision of help through services and resources available to the authority can avoid the need for court proceedings.

After completing the application form, the local authority must file it, together with sufficient copies to enable the authority to serve each respondent with a copy. The authority will therefore have to consider who are the respondents in order to know how many copies to file at court.

Respondents

To find out who are to be the respondents and, therefore, whom the local authority must serve with the application, it will have to consult Schedule 2 to the Rules. Column (iii) sets out who the respondents should be to each application under the Act. Not all the persons listed here will necessarily be respondents in every case. The column lists all possible respondents.

In the case of proceedings under section 31 the respondents are:

(a)   every person whom the applicant believes to have parental responsibility for the child

(b)   where the child is the subject of a care order, every person whom the applicant believes to have had parental responsibility immediately before the making of the care order

(c)   the child (because proceedings under section 31 are 'specified proceedings' under section 41(6)).

Written notice

The applicant must give *written notice* of the proceedings and the date, time and place of the hearing or directions appointment to:

(a)   if applicable, the local authority providing accommodation for the child (unlikely)

(b)   persons who are caring for the child at the time when the proceedings are commenced

(c)   where applicable, in the case of proceedings brought in respect of a child who is alleged to be staying in a certificated refuge, the person who is providing the refuge

(d)   every person whom the applicant believes to be a party to pending relevant proceedings in respect of the same child

(e)   every person whom the applicant believes to be a parent without parental responsibility for the child. (An obvious example would be the father of an illegitimate child who has not acquired parental responsibility in any of the ways described in chapter 7.)

Service

In the case of an application under section 31 of the Act the applicant must serve the respondents with the application at least *three* days before the hearing fixed by the clerk (see column (ii) of Schedule 2 on pages 214 and 215 of the Rules) and see chapter 2 for mode of service. Remember to file a statement of service.

Directions hearing

It is highly unlikely that the court will be in a position to decide the application for a care order or a supervision order at the first hearing. The first hearing before the court is likely, therefore, to be a hearing for directions and for an interim care order.

Before this initial hearing the applicant must address a number of specific issues:

(a)   Do we want an *interim* care order?

(b)   What *directions* do we want?

(c)   What *plans* do we have to safeguard and promote the child's welfare while the interim order is in force – in particular what sort of *placement* do we plan?

(d)   What sort of *contact* do we envisage between the child and his parents and others connected with him?

One of the most important issues at the first hearing will be the application for an interim care order.

11.5   THE COURT'S OPTIONS

The court's options at this stage are subject to the mandatory obligation imposed upon the court by section 32 which provides that the court *must* draw up a timetable with a view to disposing of the application *without delay*.

Interim care order

Jurisdiction

Section 38 provides that the court may make an interim care order when it adjourns an application for a care order (and also when it directs a local authority to investigate a child's circumstances under section 37).

Test

The court must be satisfied that there are *reasonable grounds for believing* that the child's circumstances fulfil the criteria for a full care order (section 38(2)).

This is clearly a less stringent test than for a full care order which needs *proof* that the child is suffering or likely to suffer significant harm. The reason is obvious: the evidence will simply not be available at this stage.

The welfare principle

The welfare principle and checklist apply as does section 1(5) – presumption *against* an order.

Duration

Up to *eight weeks*. The maximum period should not, however, be regarded as standard practice.

Further interim order

Further interim orders may be made.

Duration of further orders

Be careful here. If the first interim order was for eight weeks, then a second interim order may last up to four weeks. If the first interim order was for less than eight weeks then the second and any subsequent interim order can be *in total* for up to eight weeks *from the date the first interim order was made*.

Directions

Section 38(6) provides that when the court makes an interim care order (or interim supervision order) it may give such directions (if any) as it considers appropriate with regard to any medical or psychiatric examination or other assessment of the child.

Medical examination

Section 38(7) provides that the court can prohibit such examination or assessment or direct that it should take place only with the court's specific approval.

Child's refusal

As usual, if the child is of sufficient understanding to make an *informed* decision he may refuse the examination or assessment.

This is likely to be a fruitful source of jurisprudence. What constitutes understanding sufficient to make an informed decision? Must the child know of all the ramifications and consequences of his refusal? Submitting to an examination following alleged sexual abuse by a parent may provide the evidence necessary to prove the allegation, but it may also lead to the child's continued separation from a parent who is genuinely loved.

If the doctor or other examiner is aware that the child's consent is not forthcoming the appropriate action is to refer the matter to the court for further directions. The guardian's assistance in determining whether the child is of sufficient understanding to make an informed decision can then be enlisted.

Interim supervision order

Jurisdiction

Section 38 provides that the court may make an interim supervision order when it adjourns an application for a care order (and also when it directs a local authority to investigate a child's circumstances under section 37). An alternative to an interim care order might be an interim supervision order combined with a residence order. (Note that if the court is persuaded to make a residence order under section 8 as an interim measure it *must* also make an interim supervision order, unless it is satisfied that the child's welfare will be satisfactorily safeguarded without one (section 38(3).)

Test

The court must be satisfied that there are *reasonable grounds for believing* that the child's circumstances fulfil the criteria for a full supervision order (section 38(2)).

The welfare principle

The welfare principle and the checklist apply, as does the presumption *against* making an order.

Duration

As above for an interim care order.

Further interim supervision orders

As above for interim care orders.

Directions

The court's power to make directions when making an interim supervision order is the same as when making an interim care order.

Residence order

As discussed above, an alternative to an interim care order is a residence order (which must of course have attached to it an interim supervision order).

11.6   EFFECTS OF THE CARE ORDER

Duty of the local authority

Once a care order has been made the local authority *must* receive the child into its care and keep him in its care for the duration of the order (section 33(1)). It must provide accommodation for him and maintain him in other respects (section 23(1)).

The local authority can discharge this obligation by making such arrangements for the child as seem appropriate to it, including placing him with his immediate family, or any other relative or even a friend or other person connected with him (section 23).

Parental responsibility

The local authority acquires parental responsibility for the child for the duration of the care order (section 33(3)(a)). It also has the power to determine the extent to which a parent or guardian of the child may meet his parental responsibility for him (section 33(3)(b)). This power may not be exercised unless the local authority is satisfied that it is necessary to do so to safeguard or promote the child's welfare (section 33(4)).

Religion

The local authority must not cause the child to be brought up in any religious persuasion other than that in which he would have been brought up if the care order had not been made (section 33(6)(a)).

Removal from UK

As long as the care order is in force *no one* may remove the child from the United Kingdom without *either* the written consent of every person who has parental responsibility for the child *or* the leave of the court. However, the local authority may remove him for a period of less than one month. (There does not appear to be any restriction on the number of times each year the local authority may so remove him.)

Surname

No person may cause a child in care to be known by a new surname without *either* the written consent of every person who has parental responsibility for the child *or* the leave of the court.

Adoption and appointment of guardian

The local authority do not have the right:

(a)   to consent or refuse to consent to the making of an application under section 18 of the Adoption Act 1976 (freeing for adoption),

(b)   to agree or refuse to agree to the making of an adoption order, or an order under section 55 of the 1976 Act (adoption of children abroad), or

(c)   to appoint a guardian for the child.

O
Y CHA 19
E **Application for a Care or Supervision Order**
Z

Section 31 The Children Act 1989

Date received by Court

- Please use black ink. The notes on page 8 tell you what to do when you have completed the form.
- If there is more than one child you must fill in a separate form for each child.
- A care/supervision order cannot be made if the child has reached the age of 17 or is 16 and married.

- Please answer every part. If a part does not apply or you do not know what to say please say so. If there is not enough room continue on another sheet (put the child's name and the number of the part on the sheet).
- If you have any concerns about giving your address or that of the child or any other address requested in this form, you may give an alternative address where papers can be served. However, you must notify the Court of the actual address on a separate form available from the Court.

THE ▬▬ CHILDREN ▬▬ ACT

Application to The **BARCHESTER** [High] [County] [Magistrates'] Court

for a *care order *supervision order

(*delete which does not apply)

Case No.

THE ▬▬ CHILDREN ▬▬ ACT

1 About the child

(a) The name of the child is
Put the surname last.

MICHAEL DAVIS

(b) The child is a ☑ boy ☐ girl

(c) The child was born on the

5th JANUARY 1985
day   month   year

Age now **SIX YEARS**

(d) Is the child married? ☐ yes ☑ no

(e) The child usually lives at
See note on addresses at top of this form.

18 STONE TOWERS, EGDON ESTATE, BARCHESTER, WESSEX

(f) The child lives with
If the child does not live with a parent please give the name of the person who is responsible for the child.

☑ the child's mother   ☐ the child's father

(g) The child is also cared for by
Put the surname last.

TREVOR WATKINS

(h) The child is at present

☐ staying in a refuge (Please give the address to the Court separately)

☑ not staying in a refuge

(i) If the child is temporarily living away from the usual address, please say where he/she is living at present
See note on addresses at top of this form.

24, GARDEN AVENUE, BARCHESTER, WESSEX

(j) A Guardian ad litem

☑ has not been appointed

☐ has been appointed. The Guardian ad litem is

Name
Address
Tel.   Ref.

(k) A solicitor

☑ has not been appointed to act for the child

☐ has been appointed to act for the child. The solicitor is

Name
Address
Tel.   Fax   Ref.

THE ▬▬ CHILDREN ▬▬ ACT

1

2 About the applicant

(a) The applicant's full name is
Put the surname last.

(b) The applicant's title is ☐ Mr ☐ Mrs ☐ Miss ☐ Ms ☐ Other *(say here)*

(c) The applicant is **WESSEX COUNTY COUNCIL**   *local authority*

☐ an officer of the National Society for the Prevention of Cruelty to Children

☐ authorised by the Secretary of State to apply for this order

(d) The applicant's official address is
**AREA 2 OFFICES
19, THE HIGH
BARCHESTER , WESSEX**

(e) The applicant's telephone number and reference are
Tel **BARCHESTER 99520** Ref. **BM**

(f) The applicant's solicitor is
Name **THE COUNTY SOLICITOR**
Address **COUNTY HALL
BARCHESTER
WESSEX**
Tel **BARCHESTER 550** Dx. **0931 552** Ref. **JPT**

(g) The social worker is
Name **BELINDA MITCHELL**
Address **Area 2 Offices — See above**
Tel **0931 99520** Fax **0931 99524** Ref. **BM**

━━ THE ━━ CHILDREN ━━ ACT ━━

3 About the child's family

(a) The full name of the child's mother is
Put the surname last.
FIONNA DAVIS

(b) The mother usually lives at
See note on addresses at top of page 1.
**18 STONE TOWERS
EGDON ESTATE,
BARCHESTER**

(c) The full name of the child's father is
Put the surname last.
MARK DAVIS

(d) The father usually lives at
See note on addresses at top of page 1.
NOT KNOWN

(e) The child's mother and father ☐ are living together ☑ are living apart

(f) The father is ☐ married to the child's mother ☐ married to someone else
☐ single ☑ divorced

(g) The mother is ☐ married to the child's father ☐ married to someone else
☐ single ☑ divorced

2

3 About the child's family (continued)

(h) The child has

☑ no brothers and sisters under 18

☐ brothers and sisters under 18. They are

See notes on addresses at top of page 1.

Put the names, addresses and ages of all full brothers and sisters.

If the child has halfbrothers or halfsisters, stepbrothers or stepsisters say who they are in (i) below.

If there are other children who are treated as children of the family say who they are in (i) below.

The name(s) of the brother(s) and sister(s)	Age (years)	The address(es) of the brother(s) and sister(s)
N/A		*N/A*

☑ No order has been made for any brother or sister

☑ No order for a brother or sister has been applied for

Do not include adoption orders.

☐ An order has been made for a brother or sister

☐ An order for a brother or sister has been applied for

The name(s) of the child(ren)	The type of order	The court which made the order and when or which will hear the application and the case number if known	✓ if the order has been applied for	is in force
N/A	*N/A*	*N/A*		

(i) There are other children

☐ under 18 who do not live with the family

☐ under 18 who live with the family

They are: *See notes on addresses at top of page 1.*

The name of the child	The age of the child	Please give reasons why the child lives/ does not live with the family	Address of child not living with the family
NONE	*N/A*	*NONE*	*N/A*

THE ▬▬ CHILDREN ▬▬ ACT

4 Section 37(1) directions

(a) A section 37(1) direction for
the child's circumstances
to be investigated

[✓] has not been made by a Court

[ ] has been made by a Court

The Court was

N/A

The direction was made on   Case No.

━━━━━━━━━━━━━━━━ THE ▬▬ CHILDREN ▬▬ ACT ━━━━━━━━━━━━━━━━

5 Parental responsibility

Some people have "parental responsibility" for a child.
The law says what "parental responsibility" is
and which people have it. These people include:

A the mother

B the father
if he was married to the child's mother
when the child was born

C the father
if he was **not** married to the child's mother
when the child was born
   but he now has a residence order

   or he now has a court order
     which gives him parental responsibility

   or he now has a formal "parental responsibility
     agreement" with the mother

   or he has since married the mother

D a guardian of the child

E someone who holds a custody or residence order

F a local authority which has a care order

G someone who holds an emergency protection order

H any man or woman who has adopted the child

The people who have parental
responsibility for this child are
believed to be

See note on addresses at the top of page 1.

Name	Address
Fionna Davis	*18, Stone Towers, Egdon Estate, Barchester, Wessex.*
Mark Davis	*Not known.*

━━━━━━━━━━━━━━━━ THE ▬▬ CHILDREN ▬▬ ACT ━━━━━━━━━━━━━━━━

6 About other applications and orders which affect the child

(a) An Emergency Protection Order   ☑ is not in force

                                        ☐ is in force. The court which made the order was

Case No.

The Order ends on

(b) Other applications have   ☑ not been made

                                       ☐ been made or will be made

What the application was for or will be for	When an application was made or will be made	The Court which heard the application or will hear the application and the case number if known	The result
N/A	N/A	N/A	N/A

(c) Other orders   ☑ have not been made

                               ☐ have been made. The orders are

*Please include orders that have been made
but are no longer in force.*

Do not include adoption orders.

The type of order	When the order was made	The Court which made the order and the case number if known	✓ if the order has expired (say when)	is in force
N/A	N/A	N/A		

7 About this application

(a) The grounds for applying for a care/supervision order are:

*Delete one of * if appropriate.*

that the child concerned is suffering, ~~or is likely to suffer,~~ *(stet)* significant harm; *(stet)* and that the harm, ~~or likelihood of harm,~~ is attributable to *(stet)*

*the care given to the child, ~~or likely to be given to the child~~ if the order were not made, not being what it would be reasonable to expect a parent to give to the child

~~*the child's being beyond parental control~~

(b) These grounds exist because

For the last six months the child has been arriving at school in a dirty and unkempt condition. On four recent occasions he has been observed by his form teacher to have minor bruising to both legs. It is believed that the cohabitee, Trevor Watkins, is a drug abuser who is violent towards both mother and child. Mrs Davis has consistently refused to seek injunctive relief against Mr. Watkins. The applicant believes that Mrs. Davis is unable to protect Michael from further violence — and see 7 (c)

(c) If, as part of application for a supervision order, directions are requested, please give details and full supporting reasons.

Please say in part 8 what your plans are for the child and the terms of the order you are asking for.

N/A

6

7 **About this application (continued)**

(d) If you are also requesting an interim
order tick the box and delete one of *

[✓] that there are reasonable grounds for believing that
the circumstances with respect to the child are
that the child concerned is suffering,
or is likely to suffer,
significant harm;
and that the harm, or likelihood of harm, is attributable to

*the care given to the child, or likely to be given to the child
if the order were not made, not being what it would be
reasonable to expect a parent to give to the child

~~*the child's being beyond parental control~~

(e) These grounds exist because

Firstly, see 7(b) and secondly, seven
days ago the mother moved the child
to his grandmother's house, stating
that she feared for his safety at
home. Grandmother has made
it clear that she cannot look
after the child, for an extended
period.

(f) The following directions are
requested for the interim order.

Please give full supporting reasons.

(1) Appointment of a guardian ad
litem

(2) Leave to carry out a full
medical examination of Michael.
Mrs Davis has refused to take
Michael to his G.P. and the
applicant wishes to ascertain the
nature and extent of Michael's
injuries.

(g) The respondent(s) will be

● people with parental responsibility (see part 5)
● the child
● other people allowed by the Rules of Court.

Please give details below.

*(i) Only give details of those respondents
whose names and addresses have not
been given in part 5.*

*(ii) Please put the address where the
respondent usually lives or where papers
can be served. See note on addresses at
the top of page 1.*

*(iii) You will have to serve a copy of this
application on the respondents.*

The name of the respondent	The respondent's address

THE ▬ CHILDREN ▬ ACT ▬

8 The plans for the child if a final order is made

The plans for the child are

Please include the terms of the order you are asking for with supporting reasons.

Please make specific reference to arrangements for contact with the child.

(1) that the child be placed in our care

(2) We intend to work towards a speedy rehabilitation of Michael with his mother but in the absence of Mr. Watkins. We believe that Mrs Davis is capable of providing appropriate care for her son, but her relationship with Mr. Watkins is preventing her from so doing. Her persistent failure to recognise the dangers posed to Michael by the continued presence of Mr. Watkins in the home has made it impossible to work with Mrs. Davis.

(3) We propose that Michael should have daily contact with his mother but no contact with Mr. Watkins

━━━━ THE ━━ CHILDREN ━━ ACT ━━━━

9 Declaration

I declare that the information I have given is correct and complete to the best of my knowledge.

Signed *Belinda Mitchell*   Date *1st November 1991*

━━━━ THE ━━ CHILDREN ━━ ACT ━━━━

WHAT YOU (THE PERSON APPLYING) MUST DO NEXT

● There is a Notice of Hearing on page 9. Fill in the boxes on the Notice.

● Take or send this form and any supporting documentation to the court with enough copies for each respondent to be served. The top copy will be kept by the court and the other copies given or sent back to you for service.

● You must then serve the copies of the Application, the Notice of Hearing and any supporting documentation according to the Rules. You may also be required under the Rules to give notice of the proceedings to other people.

━━━━ THE ━━ CHILDREN ━━ ACT ━━━━

In the *BARCHESTER* [High] [County] [Magistrates'] Court

at *14, High Street, Barchester, Wessex*

(When writing to the Court please state the Case No.) **Case No.**

Tel. *BARCHESTER 427925* Fax *0931 427 924*

━━━ THE ━━ CHILDREN ━━ ACT ━━━

Notice of a [Hearing] [Directions Appointment]

You are named as a Respondent in these proceedings

about the child | *MICHAEL DAVIS*

☑ a boy ☐ a girl

born on the | *5th JANUARY 1985*

You must read this Notice now.

━━━ THE ━━ CHILDREN ━━ ACT ━━━

About the [Hearing] [Directions Appointment]

name of applicant

WESSEX COUNTY COUNCIL

has made an application to the Court.

The Court has been asked to make | ☑ a care order | ☐ a supervision order

━━━ THE ━━ CHILDREN ━━ ACT ━━━

To be completed by the Court

The Court will hear this at

on

at | o'clock

the time allowed is

━━━ THE ━━ CHILDREN ━━ ACT ━━━

WHAT YOU MUST DO

▶ There is a copy of the application with this Notice. Read the application now. You do not have to fill in any part.

▶ You should obtain legal advice from a solicitor or, alternatively, from an advice agency. The Law Society administers a national panel of solicitors to represent children and other parties involved in proceedings relating to the children. Addresses of solicitors (including panel members) and advice agencies can be obtained from the Yellow Pages and the Solicitors Regional Directory which can be found at Citizens Advice Bureaux, Law Centres and any local library.

▶ You may be entitled to legal aid. For certain Children Act proceedings, children, parents and those with parental responsibility will usually be eligible for legal aid automatically.

date

━━━ THE ━━ CHILDREN ━━ ACT ━━━

9

Chapter 12

Applications for Contact with a Child in Care

12.1 INTRODUCTION

There can be no doubt but that the provisions contained in the Act substantially improve the position of parents and others connected with the child who seek contact with him compared with the old law, and they limit the power of the local authority to deny contact and to control such contact.

The new provisions are almost certainly a result of the very considerable resentment and frustration experienced and voiced by those who felt that once their child had been removed by the local authority, it was often an uphill struggle to maintain contact with the child. The lack of contact frequently operated to the great disadvantage of the parents when – often many months later – final decisions were taken by the court about the future of the child.

The dice are no longer loaded in favour of the local authority.

12.2 PRINCIPLES

There are two basic principles. The first is that a local authority *must* allow reasonable contact with:

(a)   the parents

(b)   any guardian

(c)   or any person having the benefit of a residence order or care of the child under wardship immediately before the care order was made (do not forget that a residence order and wardship lapse on the making of a care order: section 91).

The second principle is that the authority *must* (unless it is not reasonably practicable or consistent with his welfare) try to *promote* contact between the child and not only his parents, but also any relative, friend or other person connected with him (paragraph 15(1) of Schedule 2).

12.3   THE PRINCIPLES APPLIED

The local authority should take reasonable steps to ensure that the child's parents, and any person who otherwise has parental responsibility for him, are kept informed of where he is being accommodated. (Correspondingly, such persons should make sure that they keep the authority informed of their address – if they fail to do so they commit a summary offence for which they can be fined.)

The authority may make payments of money to persons connected with the child to defray the costs of visiting a child in its care.

12.4   FAILURE TO AGREE

The issue of contact should be considered by the local authority before the parties go to court, at the stage when the authority is drawing up its plans for the child in respect of whom it intends to seek a care order. The local authority should discuss its plans with persons connected with the child in an effort to arrive at an agreement before the court hearing.

If the local authority and the person seeking contact with the child cannot agree about the contact, section 34(11) provides that before making a care order with respect to any child the court *shall* (so it is mandatory) consider the contact arrangements which the authority has made or proposes to make and invite the parties to comment on the arrangements.

If any person falling within the categories outlined above is dissatisfied about the proposed contact he can apply to the court for an order at any time.

12.5   UNILATERAL REFUSAL BY LOCAL AUTHORITY

The local authority may refuse contact without reference to the court if it is satisfied:

(a)   that it is necessary to do so in order to safeguard or promote the child's welfare, *and*

(b)   some sudden development has occurred which justifies the decision to refuse contact as a matter of urgency, *and*

(c)   the refusal does not last for more than seven days (section 34(6)).

12.6   REFUSAL FOR A LONGER PERIOD

If the local authority wishes to restrict contact for a longer period *or* in circumstances where it cannot satisfy the conditions laid down in section 34(6), it must make an application to the court for an order under section 34(4) authorising it to refuse to allow contact.

12.7   CHILD AS APPLICANT

The child can make an application to the court (section 34(2)). He can also apply for his contact with another person to be reduced, suspended or terminated.

The court may make such order as it considers appropriate with respect to the contact which is to be allowed between the child and any other person.

12.8   OTHER APPLICANTS

Applications for contact with the child can be made by anyone falling outside the categories mentioned above, *provided* that they obtain the leave of the court.

If any such person, having obtained leave, is dissatisfied about any proposed contact he can apply to the court for an order at any time.

12.9   THE APPLICATION

Venue

Proceedings under section 34 should be commenced in the magistrates' court (see the Children (Allocation of Proceedings) Order 1991, article 3 – for exceptions, see chapter 2 on venue).

Making the application

As with all proceedings commenced in the magistrates' court the procedure is governed by the Family Proceedings Courts (Children Act 1989) Rules 1991 ('the Rules').

Filling in the form

Fill in Form CHA 21 which is on pages 98 to 109 of the Rules. You need to file a form for each respondent and a separate form for each child in respect of whom you are seeking an order. (To make an application for permission to refuse contact with a child in care fill in Form CHA 23 which is on pages 104 to 109.) For an example of a completed Form CHA 21, see the end of this chapter.

12.10   RESPONDENTS

The respondents are:

(a)   every person whom the applicant believes to have parental responsibility for the child

(b)   every person whom the applicant believes to have had parental responsibility before the making of the care order

(c)   *the child himself*

(d)   the person whose contact with the child is the subject of the application.

12.11   SERVICE

Serve each respondent at least *three days* before the hearing or the directions appointment. For mode of service see chapter 2.

12.12   GIVING NOTICE

Look at column (iv) of Schedule 2 to the Rules on page 216. You must give *written notice* to the following:

(a)   the local authority providing accommodation for the child

(b)   persons who are caring for the child at the time when the proceedings are commenced

(c)   in the case of proceedings brought in respect of a child who is alleged to be staying in a certificated refuge, the person who is providing the refuge.

12.13   DIRECTIONS

See chapter 4.

12.14   THE WELFARE PRINCIPLE

The welfare principle and the checklist (section 1(3)) apply as does section 1(5) – the presumption against an order.

12.15   CONDITIONS

The court can attach to a contact order whatever conditions it considers appropriate (section 34(7)), such as whether the contact should be supervised, and when and where it should take place.

12.16   FREQUENCY OF APPLICATIONS FOR CONTACT

Where a person has made an application for an order, and the application has been refused, that person may not without the leave of the court make a further application for six months (section 91(17)).

12.17   APPLICATION TO VARY OR DISCHARGE AN ORDER

The court may vary or discharge any order on the application of the local authority, the child concerned, or the person named in the order (section 34(9)).

In the case of such an application the respondents will be, in addition to those respondents mentioned above, the parties to the proceedings leading to the order.

Applications for Contact with a Child in Care

O
Y CHA 21
E
Z **Application for Contact with a Child in Care**

Section 34 (2) & (3) The Children Act 1989   Date received by Court

♦ Please use black ink. The notes on page 4 tell you what to do when you
have completed the form.

♦ If there is more than one child you must fill in a separate form for each
child.

♦ Please answer every part. If a part does not apply or you do not know what
to say please say so. If there is not enough room continue on another sheet
(put the child's name and the number of the part on the sheet).

♦ If you have any concerns about giving your address
or that of the child or any other address requested
in this form, you may give an alternative address
where papers can be served. However, you must
notify the Court of the actual address on a separate
form available from the Court.

━━━ THE ━━━ CHILDREN ━━━ ACT ━━━

Application to The **BARCHESTER**   [High] [County] [Magistrates'] Court

for an order in respect of contact with a child in care

Case No.

━━━ THE ━━━ CHILDREN ━━━ ACT ━━━

1 **About the child**

(a) The name of the child is
    Put the surname last.
    MICHAEL DAVIS

(b) The child is a   ☑ boy   ☐ girl

(c) The child was born on
    the   **5th** day **JANUARY** month **1985** year   Age now **6 years**

(d) The child usually lives at
    *See note on addresses at top
    of this form.*
    **18 STONE TOWERS
    EGDON ESTATE
    BARCHESTER, WESSEX**

(e) The child lives with
    *If the child does not live with a
    parent please give the name of
    the person who is responsible
    for the child.*
    ☐ the child's mother   ☐ the child's father   **WESSEX COUNTY COUNCIL**

(f) The child is also cared
    for by
    Put the surname last.
    MR. and MRS. JENNINGS (Foster Parents)

(g) If the child is temporarily
    living away from the
    usual address, please
    say where he/she is
    living at present.
    *See note on addresses at top
    of this form.*
    **12, FIELD AVENUE
    GREATER BARCHESTER
    WESSEX**

(h) A Guardian ad litem   ☐ has not been appointed

                            ☑ has been appointed. The Guardian ad litem is

    Name **JOHN REEVES**
    Address **14, THE GROVE, GREATER BARCHESTER, WESSEX**
    Tel **BARCHESTER 83291**   Ref **JR/DAVIS**

(i) A solicitor   ☐ has not been appointed to act for the child

                    ☑ has been appointed to act for the child. The solicitor is

    Name **JAMES HODGE & CO.**
    Address **22 THE WATLINGS, LITTLE BARCHESTER, WESSEX**
    Tel **BARCHESTER 19835** Fax **N/K**   Ref

━━━ THE ━━━ CHILDREN ━━━ ACT ━━━

2 About myself (the person applying)

(a) I am

☐ the child
☐ a parent
☐ a guardian
☐ an officer of the [_____] local authority
☑ other *(say here)* _COHABITEE OF THE CHILDS MOTHER_

(b) My title is

☑ Mr ☐ Mrs ☐ Miss ☐ Ms ☐ Other *(say here)* [_____]

(c) My full name is
Put the surname last

TREVOR WATKINS

(d) Leave to make this application
Complete only if leave is required.

☐ is being sought
☑ has been given. The Court which gave leave was

BARCHESTER MAGISTRATES COURT

Date _20.12.1991_   Case No. _CHA/89_

(e) My address is
See note on addresses at top of page 1

18 STONE TOWERS
EGDON ESTATE
BARCHESTER

(f) My telephone number is   Tel. _N/A_

(g) My solicitor is

Name _PETERS AND BRYCE_
Address _25 THE WALKWAY_
EGDON ESTATE
BARCHESTER
Tel _BARCHESTER 59248_ Fax _0931 59250_ Ref _JB_

— THE ■ CHILDREN ■ ACT —

3 Details of any other applications/orders

(a) Details of any applications pending concerning the child or orders made   *(Do not include adoption orders)*

Name of Court	Date of application or date of order made and case number(s) where known	Details of application/order
BARCHESTER MAGISTRATES	ORDER MADE IN CHA/89 ON 14th NOVEMBER 1991	INTERIM CARE ORDER IN FAVOUR OF WESSEX COUNTY COUNCIL

— THE ■ CHILDREN ■ ACT —

4 | **About this application**

(a) My reasons for making this
application are

I have been living with Fiona Davis
the mother of Michael Davis, since
November 1990. During this time I
have developed a good relationship
with Michael. Despite the allegat-
ions of the local authority, I have
never ill-treated the child. Since
the care order was made I have
seen him on only one occasion.
It is my hope that he will be
returned to live with his
mother and me.

(b) I would like the Court to order that

*Give here details of the names, addresses and
relationship to the child of the person(s) who are
to have contact and the type and frequency of
contact sought.*
*(However, if any of the addresses have been given
elsewhere on this form, do not repeat but please
state where given.)*

See note on addresses at top of page 1.

that I should be allowed to visit
Michael at his foster home at
least twice a week and without
supervision.
For my address see (2) above.

5 | Respondents

The respondents will be
- the child
- those with parental responsibility
- other people allowed by Rules of Court
- those people listed in part 4b

(i) Please put the address where the respondent usually lives or can be served with papers. See note on addresses at top of page 1.

(ii) You will have to serve a copy of this application on each of the respondents.

The name of the respondent	The respondent's address
Michael Davis	c/o James Hodge & Co. 22 the Wattings Little Barchester Wessex
Fionna Davis	18, Stone Towers Egdon Estate Barchester, Wessex
Mark Davis	Unknown

THE ■ CHILDREN ■ ACT

6 | Declaration

I declare that the information I have given is correct and complete to the best of my knowledge.

Signed | *T. Watkins*   Date | *21st December 1991*

THE ■ CHILDREN ■ ACT

WHAT YOU (THE PERSON APPLYING) MUST DO NEXT

◗ There is a Notice of Hearing on page 5. Fill in the boxes on the Notice.

◗ Take or send this form and any supporting documentation to the Court with enough copies for each respondent to be served. The top copy will be kept by the Court and the other copies given or sent back to you for service.

◗ You **must** then serve the copies of the Application, the Notice of Hearing and any supporting documentation according to the Rules. You may also be required under the Rules to give notice of the proceedings to other people.

THE ■ CHILDREN ■ ACT

In the *BARCHESTER* [High] [County] [Magistrates'] Court

at *14 HIGH STREET, Barchester, Wessex*

(When writing to the Court please state the Case No.)   **Case No.**

Tel. *Barchester 427925*   Fax *0 931 427924*

━━━ THE ━━━ CHILDREN ━━━ ACT ━━━

Notice of a [Hearing] [Directions Appointment]
You are named as a Respondent in these proceedings

about the child   *MICHAEL DAVIS*

☑ a boy ☐ a girl

born on the   *5th January 1985*

You must read this Notice now

━━━ THE ━━━ CHILDREN ━━━ ACT ━━━

About the [Hearing] [Directions Appointment]   *name of applicant*

TREVOR WATKINS

has made an application to the Court.

The Court has been asked to make a contact order in respect of a child in care.

━━━ THE ━━━ CHILDREN ━━━ ACT ━━━

To be completed by the Court

The Court will hear this at

on

at   o'clock

the time allowed is

━━━ THE ━━━ CHILDREN ━━━ ACT ━━━

WHAT YOU MUST DO

▶ There is a copy of the application with this Notice of Hearing. Read the application **now**. You do not have to fill in any part.

▶ You should obtain legal advice from a solicitor or, alternatively, from an advice agency. The Law Society administers a national panel of solicitors to represent children and other parties involved in proceedings relating to children. Addresses of solicitors (including panel members) and advice agencies can be obtained from the Yellow Pages and the Solicitors Regional Directory which can be found at Citizens Advice Bureaux, Law Centres and any local library. A solicitor or advice agency will also be able to advise you as to whether you will be eligible for legal aid.

date

━━━ THE ━━━ CHILDREN ━━━ ACT ━━━

Chapter 13

Applications for an Education Supervision Order

13.1 INTRODUCTION

Section 36 of the Act creates a new kind of supervision order which may be made only on application by a local education authority. The new order is called an education supervision order ('ESO'). The idea behind the order is to ensure that the child is properly educated by putting the child under the supervision of a designated local education authority.

13.2 PRELIMINARIES

Who may apply?

The local education authority, who must consult the social services committee of the appropriate local authority before making an application (section 36(8)).

Criteria

The court may only make an order if it is satisfied that the child is of compulsory school age and is *not being properly educated* (section 36(3)).

'Properly educated'

A child is being properly educated only if he is receiving efficient full-time education suitable to his *age, ability and aptitude* and any special educational needs he may have (section 36(4)).

Beware the presumption

If a child is:

(a)   the subject of a school attendance order in force under section 37 of the Education Act 1944 which has not been complied with, *or*

(b)   a registered pupil at a school which he is not attending regularly within the meaning of section 39 of the 1944 Act,

the court will assume that he is *not* being properly educated, unless it is proved that he is (section 36(5)).

The welfare principle

The child's welfare is the paramount consideration and the checklist applies, as does section 1(5) – presumption *against* making an order.

13.3   THE APPLICATION

Venue

Proceedings under section 36 must be commenced in the magistrates' court (see the Children (Allocation of Proceedings) Order 1991, article 3 – but see chapter 2 on venue).

Making the application

As with all proceedings commenced in the magistrates' court the procedure is governed by the Family Proceedings Courts (Children Act 1989) Rules 1991 ('the Rules').

Filling in the form

Fill in Form CHA 25 (pages 111 to 117 of the Rules). For the procedure to be followed thereafter see chapter 2.

Respondents

The respondents will be:

(a)   every person whom the applicant believes to have parental responsibility for the child

(b) *the child himself.*

Service

Serve by the usual methods, a minimum of *seven days* before the hearing or directions appointment.

For mode of service see chapter 2, and remember to file a statement of service.

Written notice

Written notice of the proceedings must be given to:

(a) the local authority providing accommodation for the child

(b) persons who are caring for the child when the proceedings are commenced

(c) in the case of a child staying in a certificated refuge, the person providing the refuge.

13.4 THE ORDER

Effects of an ESO

The supervisor under an ESO is under a duty to advise, assist and befriend, and give directions to:

(a) the supervised child *and*

(b) his parents (note that a 'parent' includes any person who is not a parent of a child, but who has parental responsibility for him or care of him – see the Education Act 1944 as amended by Schedule 13 to the Act),

in such a way as will, in the opinion of the supervisor, secure the proper education of the child (Schedule 3, paragraph 12 (1)(a)).

Duty of parent

The parent of the child must:

(a) inform the supervisor of the child's address, if asked to do so

(b)   if he is living with the child, allow the supervisor reasonable contact with the child (Schedule 3, paragraph 16(2)).

Obligation of the child

An ESO may require the child:

(a)   to keep the supervisor informed of any change of address

(b)   to allow the supervisor to visit him (Schedule 3, paragraph 16(1)).

Failure to comply with directions

By the child

Where a child persistently fails to comply with any direction, the local education authority must notify the appropriate local authority who must then investigate the child's circumstances (Schedule 3, paragraph 19).

By a parent

If a parent of a child persistently fails to comply with a direction he shall be guilty of an offence which on summary conviction carries a fine.

Defences

See Schedule 3, paragraph 18(2):

(a)   all reasonable steps taken to comply with direction

(b)   direction unreasonable

(c)   compliance with a requirement or direction in ordinary supervision order renders compliance with ESO direction impracticable.

Duration

An ESO lasts for one year (Schedule 3, paragraph 15(1)).

Extension

On the application of the education authority, the court may extend the ESO. An application for an extension may not be made earlier than three months before the date on which the order would otherwise expire (Schedule 3, paragraph 15(2) and (3)). There may be more than one extension, but no single extension may be for more than three years (Schedule 3, paragraph 15(4) and (5)).

Termination

An ESO ends when:

(a)   the child ceases to be of compulsory school age

or

(b)   a care order is made (Schedule 3, paragraph 15(6)).

13.5   DISCHARGE OF ORDER

The court may discharge the order on the application of:

(a)   the child

(b)   a parent

(c)   the local education authority concerned.

If the court discharges an order, it may direct the local authority within whose area the child lives to investigate the child's circumstances (Schedule 3, paragraph 17).

13.6   CONCURRENT ORDERS

An ESO may run concurrently with a supervision order or a criminal supervision order. An existing school attendance order is discharged when an ESO is made (Schedule 3, paragraph 13(2)).

Chapter 14

Applications to Protect Children: The Emergency Protection Order

14.1 BACKGROUND

The Act contributes to the protection of children in two ways. It imposes a duty upon local authorities to investigate circumstances which signal harm to children and it creates three new orders:

(a)   the emergency protection order

(b)   the child assessment order

(c)   the recovery order.

The police too are given special powers under the new Act which they can exercise without recourse to the courts.

14.2   THE INVESTIGATIVE DUTY

A local authority *must* investigate:

(a)   when they have *reasonable cause* to suspect that a child in their area is suffering or is likely to suffer significant harm (section 47(1)(b))

(b)   when they are informed that a child in their area is the subject of an *emergency protection order* (see below) (section 47(1)(a)(i))

(c)   when they are informed that a child in their area is in *police protection* (section 47(1)(a)(ii))

(d)   when they have *obtained an emergency protection order* in respect of a child (section 47(2))

(e)   when a *court* in family proceedings *directs* them to investigate a child's circumstances under section 37(1) of the Act and also under paragraph 17 of Schedule 3 (discharge of education supervision order)

(f)   when a local education authority notifies them that a child is *persistently failing to comply* with directions given under an education supervision order (paragraph 19 of Schedule 3).

When they are investigating in the circumstances outlined in (a) to (c) inclusive above they should make such enquiries as they consider necessary to enable them to decide *whether* they should take any action to promote the child's welfare.

If they are investigating after they have obtained an emergency protection order (that is, under section 47(2)), they should make such enquiries as they consider necessary to enable them to decide *what action* they should take to safeguard or promote the child's welfare.

If the local authority are investigating pursuant to section 37(1) they must consider whether they should:

(a)   apply for a care order or a supervision order

(b)   provide services or assistance for the child or his family

(c)   take any other action with respect to the child (section 37(2)).

Help from other agencies

Section 47(9) imposes a duty upon other local authorities, local education authorities, housing authorities and health authorities to assist with enquiries.

Should the local authority see the child?

Unless they are satisfied that they have sufficient information about him they should try to see him (section 47(4)). A doctor or officer of the NSPCC could be asked by them to see the child on their behalf.

If the local authority (or those acting on their behalf) are refused access to the child concerned or denied information as to his whereabouts they should apply for either:

(a)   an emergency protection order

(b)   a child assessment order

(c)   a care order or

(d)   a supervision order

unless they are satisfied that his welfare can be satisfactorily safeguarded in some other way (section 47(6)).

This chapter deals with applications for an emergency protection order. The other orders are dealt with in subsequent chapters.

14.3   EMERGENCY PROTECTION ORDER

Emergency protection orders ('EPOs') are very similar to the old place of safety orders which were available under a number of different Acts. However, there are important differences as we shall see between the two types of order.

An EPO is an *urgent* remedy which enables a court either to remove a child from a harmful environment or to prevent his removal to a situation of harm.

14.4   WHO CAN APPLY?

Anyone (e.g., a concerned neighbour or relative, a local authority or the NSPCC) can apply for an EPO, but the court will only make the order if *the court is* satisfied that:

(a)   there is reasonable cause to *believe* that the child is likely to suffer significant harm unless he is moved to accommodation provided by the applicant (section 44(1)(a)(i)), *or*

(b)   there is reasonable cause to *believe* that the child is likely to suffer significant harm unless he stays where he is (section 44(1)(a)(ii)).

The order can, therefore, be used as both a sword and a shield.

A *local authority* who have reasonable cause to suspect that a child in their area is suffering or is likely to suffer significant harm and are, therefore, making enquiries about the child under section 47(1)(b) can apply if those *enquiries are being frustrated* because the local authority are being *refused access* and they believe as a matter of urgency that they should have access to the child (section 44(1)(b)).

The NSPCC who are making similar enquiries which are being similarly frustrated may apply.

14.5   THE APPLICATION

Preliminaries

Satisfy yourself that the circumstances merit the application. It is envisaged that most of the applications for an EPO will be made by local authorities. The circumstances most likely to provoke an application will be a reasonable belief that a child in the area of the local authority is likely to suffer significant harm if he is not removed from where he is (e.g., a home where he is being abused) or if he does not stay where he is (e.g., a hospital where he is receiving treatment).

The circumstances which might justify an application for an EPO are as varied and complex as human nature and it would be impossible and pointless to attempt an exhaustive description of them. Each case will have to be looked at individually and it will be a matter of personal judgment on the part of social workers in collaboration with other professionals including lawyers.

All the options will have to be considered and a close eye must be kept on the fact that the court must be satisfied that the criteria are met.

Venue

Proceedings for an EPO should be commenced in the magistrates' court but see chapter 2 for exceptions.

14.6   MAKING THE APPLICATION

As with all applications to the magistrates' court reference must be made to the Family Proceedings Courts (Children Act 1989) Rules 1991 ('the Rules').

Usually *ex parte*

An application for an EPO will usually be made *ex parte* because of the need to move swiftly and the possibility that in certain cases giving notice of the application to those who have control of the child may place him in greater danger. The Rules provide, therefore, that an application for an EPO may *with the leave of the justices' clerk* be made *ex parte* (Rule 4(4)).

The procedure is to contact the justices' clerk to obtain leave to make the application *ex parte*. This can be done over the telephone or at court – on the front of Form CHA 34 (see below) the following words remind the applicant that the application for an EPO can be made *ex parte*:

> Please speak to the court official immediately if you wish this application to be heard without giving notice of the application to any other party.

Filling in the form

Fill in Form CHA 34. You will find this form on pages 139 to 146 of the Rules. It is largely self-explanatory and is designed to give as much information as possible to all concerned. (An example of a completed application form can be seen at the end of this chapter.)

If you do not know the child's name then you should describe him as fully as possible.

If leave has been obtained from the justices' clerk to make the application *ex parte*, you do not have to worry at this stage about serving anyone with this form before the hearing.

The form allows you to insert any directions that you may want the court to make. So, when it is being completed you should give consideration to any directions you wish the court to make at the hearing (e.g., a medical examination of the child – see below).

14.7 THE HEARING

Single magistrate

A single magistrate may make an EPO.

Evidence

The evidence may include hearsay evidence, and the court is permitted to read reports from doctors, police officers and others.

Section 45(7) provides that regardless of any enactment or rule of law which would otherwise prevent it from doing so a court hearing an application for or with respect to an EPO may take account of *any statement contained in any report* made to the court in the course of or in connection with the hearing, or any evidence given during the hearing which is, in the opinion of the court, relevant to the application.

Criteria

You will have to satisfy the court of the matters discussed in this chapter. (For the definition of 'harm' see chapter 11.)

The welfare principle

The welfare principle applies to this application *but the checklist does not*.

No order

The court also has to apply the presumption in section 1(5) *against* the making of an order.

Directions in the order

Medical examination

Section 44(6) empowers the court on making an EPO to give such directions (if any) as it considers appropriate about contact between the child and any named person, and any medical or psychiatric examination or other assessment of the child. The court can in the order specifically direct that there is to be *no such examination or assessment* either at all or until it directs otherwise (section 44(8)).

Contact

If there is no specific direction about contact there is a mandatory obligation on the applicant to allow the child reasonable contact with:

    (a)   his parents

(b)   any person who has parental responsibility

(c)   any person with whom the child was living immediately before the making of the order

(d)   any person in whose favour a contact order is in force

(e)   any person who is allowed to have contact with the child by virtue of an order made under section 34 and

(f)   *any person acting on behalf of any of the above*, which presumably includes a solicitor (section 44(13)).

Persons accompanying applicant on execution of order

The court may direct that the applicant be accompanied by a doctor, a nurse or health visitor when he executes the order. Such a professional may advise that it is not necessary to remove the child. It should be noted that while the order authorises the removal of the child, it does not *oblige* the applicant to remove the child.

Compelling disclosure of whereabouts

The order may also include a provision compelling anyone who has information about the child's whereabouts to disclose that information if asked to do so (section 48(1)).

Removal of other children

Furthermore, if the court is satisfied that there is reasonable cause to believe that there may be another child on the premises with respect to whom an EPO ought to be made it may make an order authorising the applicant to search for and if necessary remove the other child (section 48(4) and (5)).

14.8   SERVICE OF THE *EX PARTE* ORDER

If the court makes an EPO *ex parte* the *applicant* must *serve* a copy of the order within 48 hours after the making of the order (Rule 21(8)) on:

(a)   each party

(b)   any person who has actual care of the child (or who had such care immediately prior to the making of the order)

(c)   the local authority in whose area the child lives or is found

and within 48 *hours of the making of the order* serve *each respondent* (see below, 14.11) with the application (Rule 4(4)).

14.9   FORM OF THE ORDER

The form of the EPO can be found on pages 147 to 148 of the Rules – Form CHA 35.

14.10   REFUSAL

If the court refuses to make an EPO *ex parte* it may direct that the application be made *inter partes* (Rule 4(5)).

14.11   RESPONDENTS

The respondents will be:

(a)   every person whom the applicant believes to have parental responsibility for the child

(b)   where applicable, if the child is the subject of a care order, every person whom the applicant believes to have had parental responsibility immediately prior to the making of the care order

(c)   *the child himself.*

14.12   WRITTEN NOTICE

You must give *written notice* of the application for an EPO to:

(a)   the local authority providing accommodation for the child

(b)   persons who are caring for the child at the time when the proceedings are commenced

(c)   in the case of proceedings brought in respect of a child who is alleged to be staying in a certificated refuge the person providing the refuge

(d)   every person whom the applicant believes to be a parent of the child.

14.13   EFFECT OF THE ORDER

Authorises removal

The order operates as a direction to any person who is in a position to do so to comply with any request to produce the child to the applicant, and it authorises the removal of the child to the applicant's accommodation or the prevention of his removal from where he is, including in particular from any hospital at which he is a patient.

Authorises search

The order may authorise the applicant to enter premises specified by the order and search for the child (section 48(3)). It will be usual for an applicant to seek this authorisation at the hearing and to obtain a search warrant in support.

Confers parental responsibility

The EPO gives parental responsibilty to the applicant but the applicant is only allowed to take such action in meeting that responsibility as is reasonably required to safeguard or promote the welfare of the child (section 44(5)(b)).

Examination of child

If the order directs that the child be medically or in some other way examined, can the child refuse?

Yes, if he is of sufficient understanding to make an *informed* decision about the matter.

14.14   ENFORCEMENT

What happens if a person who is directed to disclose the whereabouts of the child refuses to do so?

Contempt

His failure to comply with the direction is a contempt of court. In the county court contempt can result in committal proceedings. In the magistrates' court such failure is punishable by a fine or imprisonment under section 63(3) of the Magistrates' Courts Act 1980.

Obstruction

If a person intentionally obstructs an authorised applicant exercising his powers of search under section 48(3) and (4) he commits a criminal offence (section 48(7)) which on summary conviction carries a fine.

Assistance of a constable

If the applicant has obtained a supporting search warrant a police constable may assist the applicant, using reasonable force if necessary (section 48(9)). In any event, in a dire emergency the constable could exercise his power under section 17(1)(e) of the Police and Criminal Evidence Act 1984 to enter and search premises without a warrant for the purpose of saving life and limb.

14.15 DURATION

No more than eight days

An EPO will last as long as the court specifies but it cannot have effect for more than *eight* days (section 45(1)). However, if the eighth day is a public holiday (which includes a Sunday) the court may specify a period which ends at noon on the first day after the holiday (section 45(2)).

Extension

Section 45(4) permits a local authority (or the NSPCC) or any person with parental responsibility for the child as a result of the EPO to ask the court to extend the effect of the order for a period of up to seven days. (For the form to extend the EPO see CHA 38 on pages 154 to 157 of the Rules.)

Further extension

The order cannot be extended more than once (section 45(6)).

When will the court grant an extension?

The court may only grant an extension if it has reasonable cause to believe that the child concerned is likely to suffer significant harm if the order is not extended (section 45(5)).

14.16   CHALLENGING THE EPO

Three-day wait

The very nature of the urgent concern about the child means that most applications for an EPO will be heard *ex parte* and the order will be executed before the parents, or others against whom the EPO is sought, can be heard by the court. Accordingly, section 45(8) provides that the child, his parents, any other person who has parental responsibility or any person with whom he was living immediately before the making of the order can apply for the order to be discharged but an applicant must wait for at least *72 hours* from the time the order was made. However, the right to apply to discharge the EPO is not available to a person who was present when the order was made (section 45(11)). Nor is it possible to seek to discharge an extended order (section 45(11)(b)). The reason is that hearings to extend the EPO will be on notice and any interested party will at that hearing have had an opportunity of arguing against the extension.

Appeal

There is *no right of appeal* against the making of, or refusal to make, an EPO or *against any direction* given by the court in connection with such an order (section 45(10)).

14.17   APPLICATION TO DISCHARGE THE EPO

Form

The application is made on Form CHA 40 on pages 159 to 162 of the Rules.

Who can apply?

  (a)   the child

  (b)   a parent

  (c)   any person who has parental responsibility

  (d)   any person with whom the child was living immediately before the making of the order (section 45(8)).

O
Y **CHA 34**
E
Z
Application for Emergency Protection Order

Section 44 The Children Act 1989   **Date received by Court**

▸ Please use black ink. The notes on page 7 tell you what to do when you have completed the form.
▸ If there is more than one child you must fill in a separate form for each child.

▸ Please answer every part. If a part does not apply or you do not know what to say please say so. If there is not enough room continue on another sheet (put the child's name and the number of the part on the sheet).
▸ If you have any concerns about giving your address or that of the child or any other address requested in this form, you may give an alternative address where papers can be served. However, you must notify the Court of the actual address on a separate form which you can get from the Court office.

> Please speak to the Court official immediately if you wish this application to be heard without giving Notice of the application to any other party.

Application to The **BARCHESTER** ——— THE ——— CHILDREN ——— ACT ——— [High] [County] [Magistrates'] Court
for an Emergency Protection Order   **Case No.**
——— THE ——— CHILDREN ——— ACT ———

1 About the child

(a) The name of the child is
Put the surname last. | **JENNIFER BROOKS**

(b) The child is a | ☐ boy ☑ girl

(c) The child was born on the | **19th** day **JULY** month **1981** year | Age now **10 years**

(d) The child usually lives at
See note on addresses at top of this form. | **94, THE GREEN, BARCHESTER, WESSEX**

(e) The child lives with
If the child does not live with a parent please give the name of the person who is responsible for the child. | ☑ the child's mother ☑ the child's father

(f) The child is also cared for by
Put the surname last. | **N/A**

(g) The child is at present | ☐ staying in a refuge (Please give the address to the Court separately)
| ☑ not staying in a refuge

(h) If the child is temporarily living away from home, please say where he/she is living at present.
See note on addresses at the top of this form. | **WARD 10**
BARCHESTER GENERAL HOSPITAL
BARCHESTER, WESSEX

(i) If the child's identity is unknown state any details that identify the child.
You may attach a recent photo of the child for the use of the Court. | **N/A**

(j) A Guardian ad litem | ☑ has not been appointed
| ☐ has been appointed. The Guardian ad litem is
| Name
| Address **N/A**
| Tel.   Fax   Ref.

(k) A solicitor | ☑ has not been appointed to act for the child
| ☐ has been appointed to act for the child. The solicitor is
| Name
| Address **N/A**
| Tel.   Fax   Ref.

——— THE ——— CHILDREN ——— ACT ———

1

2 About the applicant

(a) The applicant's title is [✓] Mr [ ] Mrs [ ] Miss [ ] Ms [ ] Other *(say here)* [   ]

(b) The applicant's full name is [RONALD COWLEY]
Put the surname last.

(c) The applicant is

[ ] an officer of the [WESSEX C.C.] local authority

[ ] an officer of the National Society for the Prevention of Cruelty to Children

[ ] a designated police officer

on behalf of [   ] local authority

[ ] authorised by the Secretary of State

[ ] other *(say here)* [   ]

(d) The applicant's address is AREA 2 OFFICES
State home or office. 19 THE HIGH
BARCHESTER
WESSEX

(e) The applicant's telephone number and reference are Tel. BARCHESTER 99520   Ref. RW

(f) The applicant's solicitor is Name THE COUNTY SOLICITOR
Address COUNTY HALL
BARCHESTER

Tel. BARCHESTER 550 Fax 0931 552   Ref. JPT

THE ■■■ CHILDREN ■■■ ACT

3 About the child's family

(a) The name of the child's mother is LINDA BROOKS
Put the surname last.

(b) The mother usually lives at 94, THE GREEN
See note on addresses at the top of this form. BARCHESTER
WESSEX

(c) The name of the child's father is DAVID BROOKS
Put the surname last.

(d) The father usually lives at See 3 (b)
See note on addresses at the top of this form.

(e) The child's mother and father [✓] are living together   [ ] are living apart

2

3 About the child's family (continued)

(f) The father is
- [✓] married to the child's mother
- [ ] single
- [ ] married to someone else
- [ ] divorced

(g) The mother is
- [✓] married to the child's father
- [ ] single
- [ ] married to someone else
- [ ] divorced

(h) The child has
- [✓] no brothers and sisters under 18
- [ ] brothers and sisters under 18. They are

Put the names, addresses and ages of all full brothers and sisters.

If the child has halfbrothers or halfsisters, stepbrothers or stepsisters, say who they are in (i) below.

If there are other children who are treated as children of the family say who they are in (i) below.

See note on addresses at the top of page 1.

The name(s) of the brother(s) and sister(s)	Age (years)	The address(es) of the brother(s) and sister(s)
N/A		N/A

Do not include adoption orders.

- [✓] No order has been made for any brother or sister
- [✓] No order for a brother or sister has been applied for
- [ ] An order has been made for a brother or sister
- [ ] An order for a brother or sister has been applied for

The name(s) of the child(ren)	The type of order	The Court which made the order and when or which will hear the application. Give the case number(s) where known	✓ if the order has been applied for	is in force
N/A	N/A	N/A		

3

3 About the child's family (continued)

(i) There are other children ☐ under 18 who do not live with the family

☐ under 18 who live with the family

They are:

See note on addresses at the top of page 1

The name of the child	The age of the child	Please give reasons why the child lives/ does not live with the family	Address of children not living with the family
N/A	N/A	N/A	N/A

━━━━ THE ━━━ CHILDREN ━━━ ACT ━━━━

4 Parental responsibility

Some people have "parental responsibility" for a child.
The law says what "parental responsibility" is
and which people have it. These people include:

A the mother

B the father
if he was married to the child's mother
when the child was born

C the father
if he was **not** married to the child's mother
when the child was born
but he now has a residence order

or he now has a Court order
which gives him parental responsibility

or he now has a formal "parental responsibility
agreement" with the mother

or he has since married the mother

D a guardian of the child

E someone who holds a custody or residence order

F a local authority which has a care order

G someone who holds an emergency protection order

H any man or woman who has adopted the child

The people who have parental
responsibility for this child are
believed to be.

See note on addresses at the top of page 1.

Name	Address
LINDA K DAVID BROOKS	See 3 (a)-(a)

━━━━ THE ━━━ CHILDREN ━━━ ACT ━━━━

5 About other applications and orders which affect the child

(a) Other applications have

☑ not been made

☐ been made or will be made

What the application was for or will be for	When an application was made or will be made	The Court which heard the application or which will hear the application. Give the case no. if known	The result
N/A	N/A	N/A	N/A

(b) Other orders

☑ have not been made

☐ have been made. The orders are

Please include orders that have been made but are no longer in force.   *(Do not include adoption orders).*

The type of order	When the order was made	The Court which made the order and the case number if known	√ if the order has expired (say when)	is in force
N/A	N/A	N/A		

6 About this application

(a) The grounds for making this application are

Delete one* if it does not apply.

1 ☑ that there is reasonable cause to believe that the child is likely to suffer significant harm if
~~*the child is not removed to accommodation provided by or on behalf of the applicant~~
*the child does not remain in the place in which the child is currently being accommodated.

Only an officer of a local authority should tick box 2.

2 ☐ that enquiries are being made with respect to the child's welfare under section 47(1)(b)
and
that those enquiries are being frustrated by access to the child being unreasonably refused to a person authorised to seek access and that there is reasonable cause to believe that access to the child is required as a matter of urgency.

Only an authorised person under section 31 should tick box 3.

3 ☐ that there is reasonable cause to suspect that the child is suffering, or is likely to suffer, significant harm
and
enquiries are being made with respect to the child's welfare
and
those enquiries are being frustrated by access to the child being unreasonably refused to a person authorised to seek access and there is reasonable cause to believe that access to the child is required as a matter of urgency.

(b) These grounds exist because

Jennifer Brooks urgently requires a blood transfusion. Both parents are opposed to this procedure purely on religious grounds and this morning they threatened to remove Jennifer from hospital to the meeting house of the Zealots of the Rising Sun claiming that "prayers could save her"

(c) The applicant would like the Court to order that

If you would like the Court to give directions on
- contact
- a medical or psychiatric examination or other assessment of the child
- information on the whereabouts of the child
- authorisation for entry of premises
- authorisation to search for another child on the premises

put these here.

(1) Wessex County Council be granted an Emergency Protection Order

(2) that Jennifer Brooks may not be removed from Barchester General Hospital

6 About this application (continued)

(d) This application will be heard

☑ without notice being given to the other side

☐ with notice being given to the other side

(e) A report or relevant documentary evidence

☑ is attached

☐ is not attached

(f) The respondent(s) will be

● people with parental responsibility (see part 4)
● the child
● other people allowed by the Rules of Court.

Please give details below

(i) Only give details of those respondents whose names and addresses have not been given in part 4.

(ii) Please put the address where the respondent usually lives or where papers can be served. See note on addresses at the top of the form.

(iii) You will have to serve a copy of this application on each of the respondents.

The name of the respondent	The respondent's address
See 4	

THE ▬▬ CHILDREN ▬▬ ACT

7 Declaration

I declare that the information I have given is correct and complete to the best of my knowledge.

Signed *Ronald Cowley*   Date *2 November 1991*

THE ▬▬ CHILDREN ▬▬ ACT

What you (the person applying) must do next

● There is a Notice of Hearing on page 8. Fill in the boxes on the Notice.

● Take or send this form and any supporting documentation to the Court with enough copies for each respondent to be served. The top copy will be kept by the Court and the other copies given or sent back to you for service.

● Unless you are asking for this application to be heard without giving Notice to any other party, you **must** then serve the copies of the Application, the Notice of Hearing and any supporting documentation according to the Rules. You may also be required under the Rules to give notice of the proceedings to other people.

THE ▬▬ CHILDREN ▬▬ ACT

In the   **[High] [County] [Magistrates'] Court**

at

(When writing to the Court please state the Case No.)

Case No.

Tel.   Fax

THE ████ CHILDREN ████ ACT

Notice of a Hearing
You are named as a Respondent in these proceedings

about the child

☐ a boy   ☐ a girl

born on the

description of child if details unknown

You must read this Notice now

THE ████ CHILDREN ████ ACT

About the Hearing

name of applicant

has made an application to the Court.

The Court has been asked to make an Emergency Protection Order.

THE ████ CHILDREN ████ ACT

To be completed by the Court

The Court will hear this at

on

at   o'clock

the time allowed is

THE ████ CHILDREN ████ ACT

WHAT YOU MUST DO

▶ There is a copy of the application with this Notice. Read the application now. You do not have to fill in any part.

▶ You should obtain legal advice from a solicitor or, alternatively, from an advice agency. The Law Society administers a national panel of solicitors to represent children and other parties involved in proceedings relating to children. Addresses of solicitors (including panel members) and advice agencies can be obtained from the Yellow Pages and the Solicitors Regional Directory which can be found at Citizens Advice Bureaux, Law Centres and any local library.

▶ You may be entitled to legal aid. For certain Children Act proceedings, children, parents and those with parental responsibility will usually be eligible for legal aid automatically.

date

THE ████ CHILDREN ████ ACT

8

CHA 34

Chapter 15

Applications for a Child Assessment Order

15.1 INTRODUCTION

A child assessment order is a new order which has no real equivalent under the old law. It provides a remedy in cases where there is some concern about the child, but there is *no immediate risk* and, therefore, no justification for urgent removal, although the parents or others responsible for the child have *refused to cooperate*.

What primarily will be in mind is a medical assessment.

15.2 PRELIMINARIES

Who can apply?

Only a local authority or a person authorised under section 31. At the moment the only 'authorised person' is the NSPCC.

Criteria

The applicant must satisfy the court that:

(a) the *applicant* has reasonable cause to *suspect* that the child is suffering, or is likely to suffer significant harm. (Note here that *the court* need not have reasonable cause to suspect, but it must be satisfied that the applicant has reasonable cause to suspect. This is a much less stringent condition than for an

EPO, before the granting of which the *court* must have reasonable cause to *believe*) and

(b)   an *assessment* of the child's health or development or of the way in which he has been treated is *required* to enable the applicant to determine whether or not the child is suffering or is likely to suffer significant harm *and*

(c)   *unless* an order is obtained it is *unlikely* that the necessary assessment will be made, or be satisfactory (section 43(1)(a) to (c)).

You should advise the applicant that at the hearing it must present to the court a detailed assessment programme.

Urgency

The applicant specifically does not have to show urgency. If there is real urgency the appropriate order to apply for is an EPO.

15.3   THE APPLICATION

Venue

Proceedings for a child assessment order ('CAO') should be commenced in a magistrates' court (see the Children (Allocation of Proceedings) Order 1991, article 3, but for exceptions see chapter 2 on venue).

Making the application

As with all proceedings commenced in the magistrates' court the procedure is governed by the the Family Proceedings Courts (Children Act 1989) Rules 1991 ('the Rules').

Filling in the form

Fill in Form CHA 32 which is on pages 129 to 137 inclusive of the Rules. For an example of a completed Form CHA 32, see the end of this chapter.

You *must* file a form for each respondent and *a separate form for each child* in respect of whom you are seeking a CAO. For the procedure to be followed thereafter see chapter 2.

Respondents

The respondents are:

(a)   every person believed by the applicant to have parental responsibility for the child

(b)   if applicable, where the child is the subject of a care order, every person whom the applicant believes to have had parental responsibility for the child immediately prior to the making of the care order.

Service

Serve each respondent at least *seven days* before the hearing or the directions appointment.

For mode of service see chapter 2.

Giving notice

Look at column (iv) of Schedule 2 to the Rules on page 215. You must give *written notice* to the following:

(a)   if applicable, the local authority providing accommodation for the child

(b)   persons who are caring for the child at the time when the proceedings are commenced

(c)   where applicable, in the case of a child who is staying in a certificated refuge, the person who is providing the refuge

(d)   every person whom the applicant believes to be a parent of the child

(e)   every person whom the applicant believes to be caring for the child

(f)   every person in whose favour a contact order is in force with respect to the child.

Directions

See chapter 4.

15.4   THE HEARING

Inter partes

The application for a CAO should be heard *inter partes* because section 43(11) provides that the applicant *shall* (so it is mandatory) take such steps as are reasonably practicable to ensure that notice of the application is given before the hearing to:

(a)   the child's parents

(b)   any person who has parental responsibility

(c)   any other person caring for the child

(d)   any person in whose favour a contact order is in force

(e)   any person who is allowed to have contact with the child by virtue of an order under section 34

(f)   *and the child himself.*

The court's approach

The court's paramount consideration is the welfare of the child. The *checklist does not apply*. The presumption of *no order* unless the court considers that making an order would be better for the child applies.

The court must be satisfied by evidence of the matters dealt with above under the heading 'Criteria'.

Consent of the parents

Obviously if the parents consent, no order is necessary. Again if only *one* consents no order would be necessary because section 2(7) enables one parent to act alone.

EPO

If in the course of the hearing the court forms the view that more urgent action is necessary it may make an EPO (section 43(3)) but if it makes an EPO it cannot make a CAO as well.

15.5 THE ORDER

Duration

The order will have effect for a maximum of *seven* days beginning with the date specified in the order (section 43(5)(b)). If it becomes clear that seven days is an insufficient period within which to carry out the assessment, the authority should seek a voluntary extension. If this cannot be negotiated they should consider applying for an interim care order or supervision order with conditions.

Directions in the order

The court can make directions in the order, for example, about where the assessment is to take place, and on such matters as whether the assessment should be a joint one involving experts appointed by the child's parents or guardian *ad litem* as well as by the local authority.

Removal of child

The applicant can remove the child from his home for the purpose of the assessment only if the order so directs and only for as long as the order provides (section 43(9)).

The court should only direct that the child be kept away from home if it is necessary for the purposes of the assessment.

Contact after removal

If the court directs that the child is to be kept away from home for the purpose of the assessment the court *must* give directions as it thinks fit with regard to the contact the child is to have.

The wording of section 43(10) suggests a very strong presumption in favour of contact, if not a mandatory obligation, which is in keeping with the general policy of the Act. The subsection refers to contact that the child '*must* [not may] be allowed to have with other persons while away from home'.

Effects of an order

A CAO imposes a duty on any person who is in a position to do so to produce the child and to comply with such directions relating to the assessment of the child as are specified in the order. Further, it authorises any person carrying out the assessment to do so in accordance with the terms of the order.

A CAO does *not* give parental responsibility to the applicant.

Refusal of child

Section 44(8) provides that the child may refuse to submit to any examination or assessment *if* he is of sufficient understanding to make an *informed* decision (see *Gillick* v *West Norfolk and Wisbech Area Health Authority* [1986] AC 112).

Child in care

If there is a care order in favour of the local authority an application for a CAO is unnecessary because the authority may arrange an assessment without specific court authority.

Form of order

The form of the order is CHA 33 on page 138 of the Rules. An application to vary or discharge a CAO should be made in form CHA 55 (pages 196 to 200).

O CHA 32

Application for a Child Assessment Order

Section 43 The Children Act 1989   Date received by Court

- Please use black ink.
  The notes on page 8 tell you what to do when you
  have completed the form.
- If there is more than one child you must fill in a
  separate form for each child.

- Please answer every part. If a part does not apply or you do not know
  what to say please say so. If there is not enough room continue on another
  sheet (put the child's name and the number of the part on the sheet).
- If you have any concerns about giving your address or that of the child or
  any other address requested in this form, you may give an alternative
  address where papers can be served. However, you must notify the Court
  of the actual address on a separate form available from the Court.

THE ——— CHILDREN ——— ACT

Application to The **BARCHESTER**   [High] [County] [Magistrates'] Court

for a Child Assessment Order   **Case No.**

THE ——— CHILDREN ——— ACT

1 About the child

(a) The name of the child is
Put the surname last.

JENNIFER FAWLEY

(b) The child is a   ☐ boy   ☑ girl

(c) The child was born on
the

23rd JANUARY 1978   Age now **13 YEARS**

(d) The child usually lives at
*See note on addresses at top
of this form.*

18 MANOR PARK WAY BARCHESTER

(e) The child lives with
*If the child does not live with a
parent please give the name of
the person who is responsible
for the child.*

☐ the child's mother   ☑ the child's father

(f) The child is also cared
for by
Put the surname last.

(g) The child is at present

☐ staying in a refuge (Please give the address to the Court separately)

☑ not staying in a refuge

(h) If the child is temporarily
living away from the
usual address, please
say where he/she is
living at present.
*See note on addresses at top
of this form.*

(i) A Guardian ad litem

☑ has not been appointed

☐ has been appointed. The Guardian ad litem is

| Name |
| Address |
| Tel.   Ref. |

(j) A solicitor

☑ has not been appointed to act for the child

☐ has been appointed to act for the child. **The solicitor is**

| Name |
| Address |
| Tel.   Fax   Ref. |

THE ——— CHILDREN ——— ACT

1

2 About the applicant

(a) The applicant is   ☐ an officer of the   WESSEX COUNTY COUNCIL —local authority

☐ an officer of the National Society for the Prevention of Cruelty to Children

☐ authorised by the Secretary of State to apply for this order

(b) The applicant's full name is
Put the surname last.

JACQUELINE FRAZER

(c) The applicant's title is   ☐ Mr   ☐ Mrs   ☐ Miss   ☑ Ms   ☐ Other *(say here)*

(d) The applicant's official address is

AREA 2 OFFICES
19, THE HIGH, BARCHESTER, WESSEX

(e) The applicant's telephone number and reference are

Tel. BARCHESTER   99520   Ref. JF

(f) The applicant's solicitor is

Name THE COUNTY SOLICITOR
Address COUNTY HALL
BARCHESTER, WESSEX
Tel. BARCHESTER 550   Fax 0931   552   Ref. JPT

(g) The social worker is

Name JACQUELINE FRAZER
Address Area 2 offices — see above
Tel. 0931 99520   Fax 0931 99524   Ref. JF

▬▬▬ THE ▬▬▬ CHILDREN ▬▬▬ ACT ▬▬▬

3 About the child's family

(a) The full name of the child's mother is
Put the surname last

SYLVIA FAWLEY

(b) The mother usually lives at
See note on addresses at the top of page 1.

NOT KNOWN

(c) The full name of the child's father is
Put the surname last

GEORGE FAWLEY

(d) The father usually lives at
See note on addresses at the top of page 1.

18 MANOR PARK WAY
BARCHESTER
WESSEX

(e) The child's mother and father   ☐ are living together   ☑ are living apart

(f) The father is   ☑ married to the child's mother   ☐ married to someone else
☐ single   ☐ divorced

(g) The mother is   ☑ married to the child's father   ☐ married to someone else
☐ single   ☐ divorced

2

3 About the child's family (continued)

(h) The child has

☑ no brothers and sisters under 18

☐ brothers and sisters under 18. They are

See note on addresses at the top of page 1.

Put the names, addresses and ages of all full brothers and sisters.

If the child has halfbrothers or halfsisters, stepbrothers or stepsisters say who they are in (i) below.

If there are other children who are treated as children of the family say who they are in (i) below.

The name(s) of the brother(s) and sister(s)	Age (years)	The address(es) of the brother(s) and sister(s)
N/A		N/A

(h) *(continued)*

☑ No order has been made for any brother or sister

☑ No order for a brother or sister has been applied for

☐ An order has been made for a brother or sister

Do not include adoption orders.

☐ An order for a brother or sister has been applied for

The name(s) of the child(ren)	The type of order	The Court which made the order and when or which will hear the application. Include case number(s) where known	✓ has been applied for	if the order is in force
N/A	N/A	N/A		

(i) There are other children

☐ under 18 who do not live with the family

See note on addresses at the top of page 1.

☐ under 18 who live with the family

They are:

The name of the child	The age of the child	Please give reasons why the child lives/ does not live with the family	Address of child not living with the family
N/A	N/A	N/A	N/A

---

4 Parental responsibility

Some people have "parental responsibility" for a child.
The law says what "parental responsibility" is
and which people have it. These people include:

A   the mother

B   the father
if he was married to the child's mother
when the child was born

C   the father
if he was not married to the child's mother
when the child was born
  but he now has a residence order
  or he now has a court order
     which gives him parental responsibility
  or he now has a formal "parental responsibility
     agreement" with the mother
  or he has since married the mother

D   a guardian of the child

E   someone who holds a custody or residence order

F   a local authority which has a care order

G   someone who holds an emergency protection order

H   any man or woman who has adopted the child

The people who have parental responsibility for this child are believed to be
See note on addresses at the top of page 1.

Name	Address
George Fawley *Sylvia Fawley*	*See 3 (d)* *Not known*

━━━━━ THE ━━━ CHILDREN ━━━ ACT ━━━

5 About other applications and orders which affect the child

(a) Other applications have ☑ not been made
                            ☐ been made or will be made

When an application was made or will be made	What the application was for or will be for	The Court which heard the application or which will hear the application and the case number(s) if known	The result
N/A	*N/A*	*N/A*	*N/A*

━━━━━ THE ━━━ CHILDREN ━━━ ACT ━━━

5 About other applications and orders which affect the child (continued)

(a) Other orders ☑ have not been made

Do not include adoption orders. ☐ have been made. The orders are

The type of order	When was the order made	The Court which made the order and the case number if known	✓ if the order	
			has expired (say when)	is in force
N/A	N/A	N/A		

━━━ THE ━━━ CHILDREN ━━━ ACT ━━━

6 About this application

(a) The grounds for making this application are that

There is reasonable cause to suspect that the child is suffering, or is likely to suffer, significant harm

and

an assessment of the state of the child's health or development or of the way in which the child has been treated, is required to determine whether or not the child is suffering, or is likely to suffer, significant harm

and

it is unlikely that such an assessment will be made, or be satisfactory, in the absence of an order under this section.

(b) These grounds exist because

(Please give details of the type of assessment and other directions sought in parts 7 & 8)

For the last three months, Jennifer has exhibited disturbed behaviour at school including unprovoked attacks on other children and staff and self-mutilation. Despite numerous requests by the applicant, Mr. Farley Jennifer's father has failed to keep appointments made for Jennifer to see a psychiatrist. The applicant believes that Jennifer should be assessed by a psychiatrist as soon as possible.

5

6 **About this application (continued)**

(c) A report/relevant
documentary evidence   ☑ is attached

☐ is not attached

(d) The respondents will be   ● people with parental responsibility
● the child
● other people allowed by the Rules of Court.
Please give details below.

(i) You do not have to give the details of those respondents whose names and addresses have been given in part 4.

(ii) Please put the address where the respondent usually lives. See note on addresses at the top of page 1.

(iii) You will have to serve a copy of this application on the respondents.

The name of the respondent	The respondent's address
See part 4	

━━━━ THE ━━━━ CHILDREN ━━━━ ACT ━━━━

7 **About the assessment**

(a) The type of
assessment is

Please give a brief description of the type of assessment that will be made.

A full psychiatric assessment

7 About the assessment (continued)

(b) The assessment will be carried out by

> *Dr. Mary Austin*

(c) The assessment will take place at

> *St. Elizabeth's Hospital Barchester*
>
> Tel. *Barchester 91475* Fax *N/A*

(d) The assessment is expected to take

> *½* days

(e) The child

- [x] should not live away from home while being assessed
- [ ] should live away from home for all or part of the assessment because

(f) During any time the child will be away it is proposed that the arrangements for a contact with the child should be

The name of the person who may contact the child and the arrangements	The person's relationship to the child	Reason
N/A	*N/A*	*N/A*

7

8 **About other directions**

The applicant would
like further directions
relating to the
assessment. Include
details as to whom the
child should be
produced.

> *An order is sought that the child be produced to Jacqueline Fraser, the applicant's social worker, who will then take her to St. Elizabeth's Hospital, for the assessment to be carried out.*

THE ■ CHILDREN ■ ACT

9 **Declaration**

I declare that the information I have given is correct and complete to the best of my knowledge.

Signed *J. Fraser*   Date *5/11/1991*

THE ■ CHILDREN ■ ACT

What you (the person applying) must do next

◗ There is a Notice of Hearing on page 9. Fill in the boxes on the Notice.

◗ Take or send this form and any supporting documentation to the Court with enough copies for each respondent to be served. The top copy will be kept by the Court and the other copies given or sent back to you for service.

◗ You must then serve the copies of the Application, the Notice and any supporting documentation according to the Rules. You may also be required under the Rules to give notice of the proceedings to other people.

THE ■ CHILDREN ■ ACT

In the *BARCHESTER*

at *14 HIGH STREET*
BARCHESTER, WESSEX

(When writing to the Court please state the Case No.)

Tel. *BARCHESTER 427925*

~~Slot~~
[High] [County] [Magistrates'] Court

Case No.

Fax *0931 - 427 924*

━━━ THE ━━━ CHILDREN ━━━ ACT ━━━

Notice of a [Hearing] [Directions Appointment]

You are named as a Respondent in these proceedings

about the child | *JENNIFER FAWLEY*

☐ a boy ☑ a girl

born on the | *23 January 1978*

You must read this Notice now

━━━ THE ━━━ CHILDREN ━━━ ACT ━━━

About the [Hearing] [Directions Appointment]

name of applicant

JACQUELINE FRAZER

has made an application to the Court.

The Court has been asked to make a Child Assessment Order

━━━ THE ━━━ CHILDREN ━━━ ACT ━━━

To be completed by the Court

The Court will hear this at

on

at   o'clock

the time allowed is

━━━ THE ━━━ CHILDREN ━━━ ACT ━━━

WHAT YOU MUST DO

▶ There is a copy of the application with this Notice. Read the application now. You do not have to fill in any part.

▶ You should obtain legal advice from a solicitor or, alternatively, from an advice agency. The Law Society administers a national panel of solicitors to represent children and other parties involved in proceedings relating to children. Addresses of solicitors (including panel members) and advice agencies can be obtained from the Yellow Pages and the Solicitors Regional Directory which can be found at Citizens Advice Bureaux, Law Centres and any local library.

▶ You may be entitled to legal aid. For certain Children Act proceedings, children, parents and those with parental responsibility will usually be eligible for legal aid automatically.

date

━━━ THE ━━━ CHILDREN ━━━ ACT ━━━

9

Chapter 16

Applications for a Recovery Order

16.1 INTRODUCTION

Section 49 of the Act creates an offence of abducting a child who is either in care, the subject of an EPO or in police protection.

If anyone takes away such a child from the person (called under the section 'the responsible person') who for the time being has the care of the child, the abductor commits an offence which is punishable on summary conviction with a maximum of six months' imprisonment or a fine or both. The offence is also committed if anyone keeps the child away from the responsible person or in any way encourages the child to run away or stay away from the responsible person. In order to recover the child the court can make a recovery order.

16.2 PRELIMINARIES

Who may apply?

Only the person who has parental responsibility for the child by virtue of the care order or EPO or, where the child is in police protection, the designated officer, may apply for a recovery order (section 50(4)) .

Criteria

The court may make a recovery order where it has *reason to believe* that the child:

(a) has been unlawfully *taken away* or *kept away* from 'the responsible person' (section 50(1)(a))

(b) has *run away* or is staying away from the responsible person (section 50(1)(c))

(c) is *missing* (section 50(1)(c)).

16.3 THE APPLICATION

Venue

Proceedings for a recovery order should be commenced in a magistrates' court (see the Children (Allocation of Proceedings) Order 1991, article 3). For exceptions see chapter 2 on venue.

Making the application

As with all proceedings commenced in the family proceedings court the procedure is governed by the Family Proceedings Courts (Children Act 1989) Rules 1991 ('the Rules').

Filling in the form

Fill in Form CHA 45 which is on pages 170 to 173 of the Rules. The form consists of five sections including the declaration and is largely self-explanatory.

Ex parte

An application for a recovery order may be made *ex parte* (Rule 4(4)) and it is very likely that such applications will be made *ex parte*, in order to avoid warning the abductor or concealer of the child.

Leave of the justices' clerk must be obtained to make the application *ex parte* and that can be obtained over the telephone if necessary. If leave is granted the application form can be filed at the time when the application is made or as directed by the justices' clerk (Rule 4(4)(i)).

Court refusing *ex parte* application

If the court refuses to make the order *ex parte* it may direct that the application be made *inter partes* (Rule 4(5)), as with the application for an EPO, see chapter 14.

16.4   RESPONDENTS

Column (iii) of Schedule 2 to the Rules provides that the following persons should be respondents:

(a)   every person whom the applicant believes to have parental responsibility for the child

(b)   if applicable, where the child is the subject of a care order, every person whom the applicant believes to have had parental responsibility immediately prior to the making of the care order

(c)   the *child himself*

(d)   the person whom the applicant alleges to have effected or to have been or to be responsible for the taking or keeping of the child.

16.5   SERVICE

If the hearing is to be *inter partes* the applicant must serve the respondents to the application no less than *one day* before the hearing.

For mode of service see chapter 2 and do not forget to file a statement of service.

16.6   GIVING NOTICE

In addition to serving the respondents, the applicant must give *written notice* to the following:

(a)   if applicable, the local authority providing accommodation for the child

(b)   persons who are caring for the child at the time the proceedings are commenced

(c)   in the case of proceedings brought in respect of a child who is alleged to be staying in a refuge which is certificated, the person who is providing the refuge.

16.7 THE HEARING

The court must be satisfied that the person making the application is authorised to do so. It will hear evidence about the circumstances of the abduction or alleged retention or concealment of the child. As usual the child's welfare is the court's paramount consideration, but as with an EPO, *the checklist does not apply*. However, the presumption *against* an order does apply and so the court must be satisfied that an order is better than no order at all.

16.8 THE ORDER

After the court announces its decision the justices' clerk shall as soon as practicable make a record of any order made in Form CHA 46 (to be found at page 174 of the Rules).

Within 48 hours of the making of an *ex parte* recovery order the *applicant must* serve a copy of the order on:

(a)   each party

(b)   any person who has actual care of the child, or who had such care immediately prior to the making of the order

(c)   the local authority in whose area the child lives (Rule 21 (7) and (8)), and see chapter 2.

The recovery order must name the child and any person who has parental responsibility for the child by virtue of a care order or EPO. If the child is in police protection the order must name the designated officer (section 50(5)).

16.9 EFFECTS OF THE ORDER

A recovery order has four effects (section 50(3)):

(a)   it operates as a *direction* to any person who is in a position to do so to *produce* the child on request to any authorised person (see below)

(b)   it authorises the *removal* of the child by an authorised person

(c)   it requires any person who has information as to the child's whereabouts to *disclose* that *information*, if asked to do so, to a constable or an officer of the court

(d)   it authorises a constable to *enter* any premises specified in the order and *search* for the child, using reasonable force if necessary.

16.10   AUTHORISED PERSON

An authorised person is:

(a)   any person authorised by the court

(b)   any constable

(c)   any person who is authorised (after the recovery order has been made by the court) by a person who has parental responsibility for the child by virtue of a care order or an EPO to exercise any power under a recovery order (section 50(7)). Note that where a person is so authorised, the authorisation shall identify the recovery order and he must, if asked to do so, produce some duly authenticated document showing that he is so authorised (section 50(8)).

16.11   OBSTRUCTING LAWFUL REMOVAL

If a person obstructs another who is exercising his power to remove a child he commits an offence which on summary conviction is punishable by a fine (section 50(9) and (10)).

16.12   REFUSAL TO DISCLOSE WHEREABOUTS OF CHILD

When an authorised person requires someone to disclose information about the whereabouts of a child, the person asked cannot be excused from complying with the request on the ground that it might incriminate himself or his spouse (section 50(11)).

Chapter 17

Family Assistance Orders

17.1 INTRODUCTION

A family assistance order, made under section 16 of the Act, is a short-term remedy which is intended to give expert help to a family experiencing problems – perhaps in the immediate aftermath of divorce. It has similarities to the old form of supervision order.

17.2 PRELIMINARIES

Who can apply?

There is no applicant: only the court can make the order.

Criteria

The court may make the order where:

(a)   it has power to make a Part II order *and*

(b)   the circumstances of the case are exceptional *and*

(c)   it has obtained the consent of every person to be named in the order other than the child (section 16(3)).

Note that the court only needs the power to make a Part II order; it does not have to make such an order.

The welfare principle

The child's welfare is the paramount consideration. *The checklist does not apply*, but section 1(5) – the presumption of no order – does apply.

17.3   THE ORDER

The order requires either a probation officer or an officer of the local authority to be made available to 'advise, assist and (where appropriate) befriend' any person named in the order (section 16(1)).

Who may be named in the order?

(a)   any parent or guardian of the child

(b)   any person with whom the child is living or in whose favour a contact order has been made

(c)   *the child himself* (section 16(2)).

17.4   DIRECTIONS IN THE ORDER

An order may direct any person named therein to take such steps as may be specified to enable the officer to be kept informed of the address of any named person and to be allowed to visit him (section 16(4)).

17.5   DURATION

The order lasts for six months unless a shorter period is specified (section 16(5)).

Chapter 18

Secure Accommodation Orders

18.1 INTRODUCTION

Section 25 of the Act governs the keeping or placement of children in accommodation provided for the purpose of restricting liberty.

The rules are broadly similar to those which were contained in the Child Care Act 1980 and the former Secure Accommodation Regulations (now repealed).

New regulations now apply, namely, the Children (Secure Accommodation) Regulations 1991 ('the Regulations') and the Children (Secure Accommodation) (No. 2) Regulations 1991 ('the No. 2 Regulations').

Changes include the extension of the secure accommodation provisions to children accommodated by health or local education authorities, National Health Service trusts and children in residential care homes, nursing homes or mental nursing homes.

As before, placement of a child in secure accommodation will be a matter of last resort.

18.2 PRELIMINARIES

Who can apply?

(a) the local authority looking after the child (Regulation 8)

(b)   the health authority, National Health Service trust, or local education authority providing accommodation for the child (unless the child is being looked after by the local authority) (the No. 2 Regulations)

(c)   the person carrying on the residential care home, nursing home or mental nursing home in which accommodation is provided for the child (again, unless the child is looked after by a local authority) (the No. 2 Regulations).

Criteria

A child *cannot* be placed and, if placed, *cannot* be kept in secure accommodation *unless* it appears that:

(a)   he has a history of absconding and is likely to abscond from any other 'description of accommodation' *and*

(b)   if he absconds, he is likely to suffer significant harm

or

(c)   if he is kept in any other description of accommodation he is likely to injure himself or any other person (section 25(1) of the Act).

The welfare principle

The welfare principle applies, as does the presumption *against* making an order. The section 1(3) *checklist does not apply*.

'Detained' and 'remanded' children

A child:

(a)   detained under section 38(6) of the Police and Criminal Evidence Act 1984, *or*

(b)   remanded to local authority accommodation under section 23 of the Children and Young Persons Act 1969 (but *only* where the child is charged with or convicted of an offence imprisonable in the case of a person aged 21 or over for 14 years or more *or* where the child is charged with or convicted of an offence of violence or has been previously convicted of an offence of violence),

cannot be placed and, if placed, *cannot* be kept in secure accommodation *unless* it appears that 'non-secure' accommodation is *inappropriate* because:

(a)   the child is likely to abscond from such other accommodation, *or*

(b)   the child is likely to injure himself or other people if he is kept in any such other accommodation (Regulation 6).

To which children does section 25 not apply?

Section 25 *does not apply* to:

(a)   a child detained under any provision of the Mental Health Act 1983

(b)   a child in respect of whom an order has been made under section 53 of the Children and Young Persons Act 1933 (punishment of certain grave crimes)

(c)   a child accommodated under section 20(5) of the Act (accommodation of persons over 16 but under 21)

(d)   a child kept away from home under a child assessment order

(Regulation 5).

Who is a child 'looked after by a local authority'?

A child who is in the care of a local authority or provided with accommodation by the authority in the exercise of any functions which stand referred to their social services committee (section 22(1) of the Act).

18.3   THE APPLICATION

Venue

Proceedings for a secure accommodation order should be in the magistrates' court (Children (Allocation of Proceedings) Order 1991, article 3). See chapter 2 on venue for exceptions.

Making the application

As with all proceedings commenced in the magistrates' court, the procedure is governed by the Family Proceedings Courts (Children Act 1989) Rules 1991 ('the Rules').

Filling in the form

Fill in Form CHA 17 (pages 82 to 86 of the Rules).

Respondents

The respondents will be:

(a)   every person whom the applicant believes to have parental responsibility for the child

(b)   where the child is the subject of a care order, every person whom the applicant believes to have had parental responsibility immediately prior to the making of the care order

(c)   *the child himself* (Rule 2(2)).

Giving notice

Written notice of the hearing must be given to:

(a)   persons who are caring for the child at the time when the proceedings are commenced

(b)   if a child is staying in a certificated refuge, the person providing the refuge.

Service

Serve *one day* before the hearing or directions appointment.

For mode of service see chapter 2.

18.4   THE HEARING

Legal representation of the child

The court must not make an order in respect of a child who is *not* legally represented in court, unless, having been informed of his right to apply for legal aid and having had the opportunity to do so, he refused or failed to apply (section 25(6)).

Reports

The justices' clerk must, if practicable, arrange for copies of all written reports to be made available to:

(a)   the applicant

(b)   the parent or guardian of the child

(c)   any legal representative of the child

(d)   the guardian *ad litem*

(e)   the child, unless the justices' clerk or the court otherwise directs (Rule 26).

Interim orders

The court may, when adjourning the hearing of an application, make an interim secure accommodation order (section 25(5)).

18.5   THE ORDER

Time-limits generally

The maximum period beyond which a child may not be kept in secure accommodation *without* the authority of the court is an aggregate of *72 hours* (whether or not consecutive) in any period of 28 consecutive days.

Time-limits on court's authorisation

The maximum *initial* period for which a court may authorise a child to be kept in secure accommodation is *three months* (Regulation 11).

The court may from time to time authorise a child to be kept in secure accommodation for *a further period* not exceeding *six months* at any one time (Regulation 12).

Remanded children

In respect of remanded children, the maximum period is the period of the remand and any period shall not exceed 28 days without further court authorisation (Regulation 13).

Form of order

The order is made in form CHA 18 on page 87 of the Rules.

18.6   PARENTAL RESPONSIBILITY

A person who has parental responsibility for a child may at any time remove the child from accommodation provided by or on behalf of the local authority, since section 25 is expressed to be subject to section 20(8) of the Act.

Chapter 19

Appeals from the Family Proceedings Court

19.1 THE GENERAL RULE

You should appeal to the High Court against:

(a)   the *making* by the magistrates of any order under the Act

(b)   any *refusal* by the magistrates to make an order under the Act (section 94(1)).

19.2 NO APPEAL

You *cannot* appeal against:

(a)   a decision by a magistrates' court to decline jurisdiction because it considers the case can be more conveniently dealt with by another court (section 94(2))

(b)   an interim periodical payments order made under Schedule 1 (section 94(3))

(c)   the making of or refusal to make an EPO (or any direction given in connection with such an order) (section 45(10)

(d)   the refusal by a magistrates' court to transfer proceedings under article 7 of the Children (Allocation of Proceedings) Order 1991 (for the procedure to be followed upon such a refusal see chapter 3).

19.3   WHAT THE HIGH COURT CAN DO

The appellate court can make *any order* it deems necessary (including incidental or consequential orders), and can direct that the case be *reheard* by the magistrates' court.

19.4   PERIODICAL PAYMENTS APPEALS

On an appeal against the making of a periodical payments order under Schedule 1, the High Court may:

(a)   order that its determination of the appeal shall have effect from a specified date (section 94(6)) and

(b)   if it reduces the payments or discharges the order, direct *repayment* or *remit* arrears (section 94(8)).

19.5   ENFORCEMENT

For the purposes of the enforcement, variation, revival or discharge of orders, any High Court order made on appeal shall be treated as if it were a magistrates' court order (section 94(9)).